jeanette d

dreams
of a Farmer's Wife

iUniverse, Inc.
Bloomington

dreams of a Farmer's Wife

iUniverse books may be ordered through booksellers or by contacting:

iUniverse
1663 Liberty Drive
Bloomington, IN 47403
www.iuniverse.com
1-800-Authors (1-800-288-4677)

Because of the dynamic nature of the Internet, any web addresses or links contained in this book may have changed since publication and may no longer be valid. The views expressed in this work are solely those of the author and do not necessarily reflect the views of the publisher, and the publisher hereby disclaims any responsibility for them.

Any people depicted in stock imagery provided by Thinkstock are models, and such images are being used for illustrative purposes only.

Certain stock imagery © Thinkstock.

ISBN: 978-1-4620-6649-0 (sc)
ISBN: 978-1-4620-6650-6 (e)

Printed in the United States of America

iUniverse rev. date: 11/22/2011

In appreciation

～～～～～

To Peggy Hedden Eiland who took time from her busy schedule to edit my book. Peggy is a graduate of Louisiana College with a major in English and a dear friend.

To Doyle, Twila and Barry who contributed their stories of growing up in the country and the experiences they encountered as children and young adults.

To my friend, Dr. Dolores Cooper who advised and assisted by sharing her computer knowledge.

In Memory of Susan Rawls Baker and Bill Rawls of Lee Drug Store and in Honor of Lee Racine from Racine Feed Store, Margie Ard of Ard's Printing and Patti Middleton of Celebrations for making my books available to local residents.

Ryan Family on the Farm

(F) Hannah, Josh, Charlene, Christina, Whitney, Grandma, Neal and Heather. (B) Noah, Barry, Joshua, Doyle, Grandpa, Maggie, Sean and Twila.

A Dyess Family Reunion in Loxley, Alabama in 1998

(F)Charlene, Sean, Heather, Hannah and Jeanette Ryan, Dianne Dyess, Joshua Bilon, Justin Davenport, Twila Bilon and Rachel Dyess (B) Barry, Noah, Whitney. Christina and John Ryan. Steve, Ethel, Bernard and Ernest Dyess.

Dedication

〜〜〜〜

I dedicate these stories to my husband, John, a city boy, who arrived in Baldwin County in 1946 with his mother and not much more than the clothes on his back, a few homing pigeons and a dog named Shep. After serving his country for four years he chose a career as a Master Mechanic at an Air Force Base in Alabama and later at a Navy Base in Florida. Having grown up in cities he observed the farmers in the area and as time passed was able to purchase a few acres of land at a time. He gradually learned the techniques of farming mainly through trial and error. Eventually, he farmed almost 200 acres as his second job while he consistently put in long hours at his Civil Service job which lasted 29 years. In his younger days he traveled to other states when extra assistance was needed to repair airplanes for prompt service. He is proud to say he has worked on the Navy's Blue Angel airplanes and the Air Force's Thunder Birds. He saved money from these trips in order to be able to purchase land to farm. When he started experimenting with small crops of sweet potatoes, corn and cucumbers, he was hooked for life and later moved on to plant larger crops. Riding his tractor became his passion and therapy. Now that he is up in age he rents the land he does not use for pasture to a young farmer. His pastime of raising chickens, homing pigeons, tending a garden and pasturing a few cattle keeps him busy. The farm will be passed on to our children and grandchildren who do not want to farm, but will have a place to hunt, fish and eat the fruit from the many trees he recently planted.

This book is also dedicated to my brother Bernard Dyess and his wife, Ethel who farmed for a living for many years. Bernard not only farmed the land by planting large crops of soy beans, corn and peanuts, but also raised cattle and hogs. Ethel worked faithfully by his side assisting in any way she could. When they surrendered everything to the Lord in order to go into the ministry, they gave up life as they knew it on the farm, counting it not as loss but as gain. Now retired from pastoring and preaching the Word, Bernard tends their muscadine vineyard and plants a large garden to have vegetables to share with their neighbors and family. Ethel still helps with his gardening. God has blessed their commitment to Him.

And I dedicate it also to my youngest brother, George Marion Dyess, the real outdoorsman of the family. Wherever he goes he hardly ever fails to bring home plenty of fish. He and his son, Greg, own our Daddy's old home place which now serves as a camp house where they hunt deer. Marion planted a pecan orchard and keeps the memories of days gone by alive. In his senior years, God has given him a talent of composing Gospel songs that he and his daughter, Gina record.

And lastly, to the Farmers of America, I would also like to dedicate these stories of the ups and downs of farming to the families who continue growing the crops even though it is sometimes more profitable to sell the land. In South Alabama cotton is again King, peanuts are profitable, and corn, wheat, soybeans and millet feed the people and livestock of our land. May God bless the efforts of the farmers and their families as they provide food and clothing for America as well as other nations of the world toiling by the sweat of their brow.

Contents

Preface

A plaque hangs over my kitchen window that reads, "Dream, Believe, Achieve." I consider myself big at dreaming, but sometimes fall short in believing I will ever achieve my goals. The first thing I do each morning is open the window blind to peek out and see if there are any cardinals or other birds at the feeders. Sometimes I have the pleasure of watching the birds as they partake of their breakfast and flutter around the yard, but other times I am disappointed that I missed their visit. I suppose that is life. At times we are enchanted by what comes our way and other times we feel let down. I have been a dreamer my entire life, but never believed that I could achieve much during my lifetime. Yet somehow God has given me a measure of confidence the last few years that has helped me have more faith in myself so I could achieve my dream of publishing two books. One is a book of historical facts and the other is a memoir that ended when I married my husband, John.

I have experienced great pleasure as I shared these books with others that have become friends that I cherish. I have also enjoyed their fellowship. Relatives that I had never met have called or written notes making it a joyful occasion when we were able to meet and find that we had so much in common.

So, while these memories are still fresh on my mind and with the help of the Lord and hopefully others, I will begin the third edition of the stories of my life. Knowledgeable and gifted people inspired and assisted me while volunteering their skills as I compiled the other books, so I am praying for workers in the field to come forth now as I relive past experiences of dreams that were fulfilled.

As I began writing this book it occurred to me that there were many years in my family's life that were unaccounted for and other stories that had not been penned concerning happenings not told after I composed my last book. Since I want to complete the events of these years for my children and grandchildren and others who come after me, my writings would not seem complete unless I write other short stories of momentous occurrences of those in-between years. Our offspring needs to know their ancestors worked diligently in hopes life would be easier for them and they would have opportunities not afforded us. I like to envision my grandchildren in the future, reading stories to their little ones about their parents' and grandparents' way of life and their activities when they were young.

Our way of life was not an easy one. Our parents had no inheritance of any kind to bequeath us. In fact it was the other way around; we supported our parents in any way we could. During our early married life we made ends meet by working hard in order to get by. We stopped buying on credit unless it was a vehicle or tractor. When the children came along we saved every way we could in order to provide what they needed but not everything they wanted. I have no regrets that we had to live on a tight budget. I did the best I could to keep my family fed, clothed, clean and happy. There was never much free time when the children were growing up but we lived life to the fullest. We did take time off to go on a couple of vacations that we enjoyed. We were living the American dream of owning a few acres to farm. Life was generally good because God was good and always met our needs.

Acknowledgements

~~~~~~~~~~~~

I would like to acknowledge all the farmers' and their wives that I have known who worked so diligently to provide food for their family as well as for this country. I also want to thank my husband, John, who was a farmer and realized what hard work was all about. John farmed the land and put in many long hours of hard labor. I was always working beside him helping and assisting in any way I could. We stretched the income to see that our family's needs were met and the bills paid even if it was what we referred to as "living from payday to payday." Besides my household duties of cleaning and cooking huge meals for the hired workers and my famished family, I still found time to be a hostess at PTA or a room mother for my children's school class. I never refused to host a meal for the visiting revival preachers or cook for the sick and bereaved in our community. All work ceased on Sundays and we went to church together as a family. John and I both taught children's Sunday school and Training Union classes at night.

I remember the mornings when I would be making our bed and gaze out the window at a field of waist-high corn stalks drying up from drought. I became accustomed to standing on the front porch looking for a tiny dark rain cloud in the sky as I prayed for rain when the heat and drought of summer caused the corn to burn and the soybeans to wither as the nematodes attacked their root system. Those were the lean years. I felt as if all of Johnny's hard work had been in vain when the crops failed.

On the other hand there were good years and I fondly look back to the time when the rains came, the crops flourished, and the market prices were advantageous so that there was sufficient income to pay off the fertilizer and seed bills and have a small profit left. Usually our garden produced enough for our needs or overly produced so we could share with others. It gave me great satisfaction to see the pantry lined with jars of food I had canned and to have fresh tasting vegetables from the freezer for the winter months. I enjoyed preparing meals for company and family dinners during these plentiful productive years.

I have walked in the farmer's wife's shoes during the productive times and also during the times of adversity and crop failures. I understood my neighbors and their family member's pain and tears when their family home and farmland went into foreclosure and knew that if not for the grace of God it could have been our home, our property. Our family had to hold fast to the thought that the soil would once more be productive and realize that God would restore what was lost if we depended on His guidance. We had to have faith and believe He would bless us if we continued to serve Him and work hard. As I look back over the years, I would like to share my faith and dreams as a farmer's wife as well as the times I had to be patient until my dreams and goals unfolded. *Jeanette*

I was continually reminded of the Parable of the Sower and other Scripture:

"See how the farmer waits for the precious fruit of the earth, waiting patiently until it receives the early and latter rain." James 5:7b

The Last Chapter

The clock is ticking, time is wasting and the years are flying by,
Stories not written now, will never be read
When my name is called and my breath is gone
There will be no more time for words unsaid
So I hang up my broom and turn off the T.V.
And pray I don't have to answer the phone.

I never intended to leave the last chapter of my life unfinished.
I prayed for opportunity to share more of my experiences,
So after the well went dry for a time and the fire dimmed low
Suddenly a spring of water, cool and refreshing began to flow.
Then little sparks of fire began glimmering and started to glow
As if stars were falling from the sky or perhaps fireworks exploding.

May the springs of water give life and the sparks of inspiration linger
So all the stories that live in my heart are penned by my fingers
Then when there are no more old tales that need to be told
From my fading memory before thoughts grow cold
I will rest my mind when the last chapter of the book unfolds
And be content knowing I have finally reached my goal.

Jeanette Dyess Ryan "The Farmer's Wife"

Introduction
Why Men Farm

Hay Harvesting Time

As a child I often wondered why men choose farming as a means of making a living for their family. I witnessed first hand how diligent my relatives and their children worked in order to bring the crops from the fields to the markets. I especially observed how hard the farmer's wives worked from dawn until after the family was fed and the kids put to bed at night. But I never thought I would ever become a farmer's wife or that my husband would operate a farm. I thought I would have been happy living in a nice house in the suburbs of a small town with nothing to do but visit with next door neighbors for coffee every morning after my housework was done. However, my spouse had other ideas. He often visited the local farmers and learned the techniques of farming. A few years into our marriage, he gradually started taking the plunge by planting small crops. After producing his first small crop he was hooked on farming. Farming at first was like a hobby until suddenly before we realized it, tilling the land had become a second job. I had become a farmer's wife without any warning. I often thought about how taking care of God's garden was man's first occupation and how God put Adam in the "Garden of Eden" to tend and keep it. However, when Adam and Eve disobeyed God and sinned, He drove them out of the garden. God told Adam that in toil (by the sweat of his brow) he would eat bread. We know that one of their sons became a farmer and the other a sheep herder. If man was to survive, then he must grow food to feed his family.

I have come to the conclusion that a true farmer is born with farming in his blood. One reason I think men enjoy farming is because they take pleasure in watching the crops grow and being outdoors, plus they like the challenge of the results of producing good crops. At times farming conditions can be brutal. If not for the bountiful supplies of rewards when the farmer is blessed with a good year no one would want to farm. I do know that when my husband is on his tractor and out on the farm that is when he is the happiest. Men like the open fields and outdoor work because they do not like to be cooped up in a house. Yes, farming can be hard dedicated work but it can also be rewarding and relaxing. Farming has always been the livelihood of our nation and the way we feed our families and people of other countries.

At one time, the small farmer grew the food to feed people, but with modern farm equipment and vast acres of land farming has now become big business. I would say that we would not be able to survive if no one chose to plow the earth and provide our food. As the wife of a farmer, I have seen the crops thrive and yield a good harvest just as I have observed them wither and dry up without rain.

I sometimes feel the same way when there are days when I have time to compose stories in order to complete this book but other days it seems I am in a dry hole and nothing appears to relay what I want to pen. I suppose when there is no inspiration I must remember to wait upon the Lord until He gives me the words just as he brings forth good fruit in due time. God's timing and my ability to write must be intertwined. As I started putting these short stories together the figs, blueberries, and citrus trees were almost ready for picking. As I write today, the vegetable garden that our family planted, watered and fertilized is withered from lack of rain and the pasture where the cattle graze has turned brown. There will be no fruit or vegetables produced from the labor of my families work unless God sends the rain showers from heaven to help it grow. This spring was the driest I can remember. We will plant another garden in late summer and wait for its yield. Yet we do not worry about the future because there are people in our state who have suffered tornadoes and lost everything so we feel blessed to still have our homes and livestock unharmed. We know that it rains on the just and the unjust so we will be content, no matter what comes our way and wait for a better crop next time.

"Inspiration…who can say where it is born, and why it leaves us? Who can tell the reasons for its being and not being? Only this…I think inspiration comes from the heart of heaven to give the life of wings, and the breath of divine music to those of us who are earthbound."

Margaret Sangster
Words from *Harvest of Gold*. Copyright Ernest R. Miller

1
The Little House Down the Lane

Two Women: One Small House

Our first Log Cabin Home

It had been a warm Sunday afternoon in 1951. My fiancé's face was beaming as he drove down the lane to show me the little house and ten acres of land that he had purchased to be our future home after we married. I did not let him know I was not as enthused as he was because I had hoped for more than a four room cabin that had been built of logs and covered with rough lumber. I began thinking about how cold this house would be in the winter as I compared it to the log cabin where I was born. As I gazed intently at the little house sitting in a yard of Bahia grass that needed mowing, it appeared that the house was lop-sided. I surmised that at least one coat of white paint had been applied to the boards that were now beginning to peel. Once inside I met the former owners who were packing to leave. Somehow, I clearly recall that all the wife was cooking for supper was some fried okra. I realized they were experiencing hard times too. I stared first at the worn linoleum that showed the imprint of the uneven flooring and then at the ceilings that were so low a tall man would surely break the bare light bulb hanging there if he failed to duck his head. I knew Johnny and his mother needed a place to live but I was not impressed the first time I viewed the little white house on a dead-end dirt road. I had been accustomed to not having indoor plumbing but had dreamed that our first home would at least have a bathroom. No, there was no elation in my heart that afternoon, but Johnny's mother was very happy. She had lived in this house with her daughter and son-in-law when Johnny was in the service so she was anxious to move in and set up housekeeping again.

The next year on a beautiful sunshiny day I married my husband, John William Ryan in a simple ceremony after church. The date was June 29, 1952. After a short honeymoon to Florida we returned to my former home to pick up my few belongings. We had very little money to waste on motel bills when we needed to stock up on groceries for the week. We had to get settled in the house before Johnny went back to work. We picked up the new Lane cedar chest which was a graduation gift from Daddy and my step-mother, Blannie. It was filled with wedding gifts such as sheets, towels and cooking utensils that would be so useful.

The morning after our first night together in the little house, I awoke with a soft breeze blowing over me as I lay in our new metal book-case bed. I was happy when I learned that my husband-to-be had installed a large window fan in our bedroom. That fan would generate quite a bit of air when another window was opened somewhere in the house. After a switch on the fan was flipped it would pull air into our room. The fan was such a blessing because it helped us to sleep better after we got used to the roar. I knew the temperature would soar in the little four room house in the summer without it. However, I had spent many hot summer nights in my bedroom in the red-roofed house I called home. There was only one window in my little pink bedroom. I sometimes slept at the foot of the bed without any cover. I closed my bedroom door because Mama and Daddy slept in the next room and I could hear Daddy snoring. Sometimes he would get up at night when the buzzing mosquitoes had found their way though the holes in the screen. Daddy kept his little spray gun filled with fly spray under his bed and I could hear him swish, swish, swish as he aimed his weapon around the bed to rid his room of the pesky insects. I never decided which was worse, the buzzing, biting mosquitoes or the terrible scent of fly spray.

I finally opened my sleepy eyes, sat up in bed and gazed at my new surroundings. Then it hit me. I suddenly realized Johnny and I had married and had spent our first night at the little white house down the lane. Johnny had also purchased a few other pieces of furniture such as a pretty blue chrome dinette table with six chairs, a refrigerator and the bookcase bed and mattress on credit when he and his mother set up housekeeping after he received his discharge from the Air Force. Since his mother had lived with his sister while he was away in the service for four years he felt it was his turn to take on the responsibility of taking care of her now that he had a place. During those years, she received a small allotment from his meager Air Force pay check but he thought he could now make more money cutting and hauling paper wood. He told me later he decided not to make the Air Force his career so he could get married and also take care of his mother.

In 1946 while in Louisville, Kentucky, Johnny's father, John William Ryan, Sr., passed away suddenly. After Mr. Ryan returned home from work at L & N Railroad, he sat down in a chair and never spoke a word. He had received his paycheck that day but his wallet was empty. He became unconscious and ended up dying 12 days later in the hospital, never regaining consciousness. Without Mr. Ryan's income, Johnny and his mother were left without monetary support except for the small jobs Johnny could pick up so they came to Baldwin County, Alabama to be near family.

After Johnny returned from California and was stationed at Brookley AFB, Ruth and Otto sold their little house and moved to a larger one. Johnny was able to buy their former home along with five acres of land from the new owners. He also purchased an additional five acres of land which joined his present land from a neighbor for $500 while he was in the Air Force.

I began to wonder where Johnny was as I meandered my way to the small kitchen of the four room cottage. I soon found a note on the table that read, "I have to run to town. You were sleeping so peacefully I hated to wake you. Love, Johnny." I walked through the other two rooms of the house we would share with Johnny's mother. She had moved her belongings and a twin bed to the front room in order for us to have the larger bedroom. The middle room would serve as a sitting room when we were able to buy furniture. We had two weeks of privacy before his mother returned from her stay with his other sister, Elsie, and her family in Pensacola. I began to wonder how the situation of two women in one small house would work out. I had always been told that no house was large enough for two women, but I would do my best to cultivate a good relationship. An old saying states, "There is only one queen bee in a beehive." I knew there could be troublesome times ahead and prayed I would be able to overlook circumstances that might upset me.

I was already upset with my dad and step-mother because they would not allow me to inherit Mama's treadle Singer sewing machine. I cried when Daddy said they needed it so Blannie could patch his work pants and I knew they did need it, but I wanted it because it had belonged to Mama. I also wanted to continue learning to sew my clothes. I knew I would someday be able to buy a sewing machine and began to feel ashamed that I had made such a scene. I suppose the real reason was I resented my step-mother having something special that had belonged to my mother. Leaving my thoughts of the past, I prepared my breakfast and began to think about how I could fit my things in our one small closet which currently held two large tool boxes that had once belonged to Johnny's father. It was getting late so I ate my cereal, dressed and prepared to clean and arrange the room. So much for a home cooked breakfast together on the first day in our new home.

At the end of the two week honeymoon, Mrs. Ryan returned from Florida and settled in. I felt that in her opinion I was incapable of running a house even though I had done all the cooking and cleaning for Daddy and my two brothers after Mama passed away. When she told me one day she was going to defrost her refrigerator, I knew where I stood, but I kept quiet. Yet that was the beginning of a silent resentment that would eat at me for years before conditions improved.

I did not respond to the refrigerator comment, but knew that Johnny purchased most of the furniture from Matthews Furniture

Store in Robertsdale in anticipation of our marriage. It was a silly little statement that I should have ignored. He told me he was going to work hard and save so that one day he would be able to build me the house of my dreams. I have to admit that I was so materialistic that those words put a dream in my heart I would keep until it became a reality. I suppose having to do without, and being raised poor, made me that way. I now know it is wrong to treasure things on this earth, but I was too young to realize that if God wanted us to have a better house in the future He would provide it some day if I would be patient. So for now I would be content in the house God provided.

When we married Johnny was working long hours harvesting timber. We referred to his job as a pulp wood harvester. I learned to drag myself out of bed at four in the morning to cook my new husband a hearty breakfast. While he ate I packed his metal lunch box with lots of fried bologna sandwiches with mustard so it would not spoil in the heat. His dome shaped lunch box was equipped with a thermos jug secured on one side. In the summer months I filled it with cold tea, but in the winter I heated vegetable soup or beans left over from supper.

Even though Johnny was slim, he worked as hard as the other men cutting down the pine trees, splitting them in lengths and loading them on the paper wood trucks. There was very little profit in this industry. I was extremely upset the day Johnny got rid of the Ford convertible. That 1946 Ford had been a dependable car before and after marriage and I hated to see it go. We found that this new adventure of Johnny being his own boss brought on extra debt because of the many ruined tires and repair bills. If not for Lon Cooper, our neighborhood grocer, letting us charge groceries at the little store in Elsanor and the timber company allowing him to charge his gasoline from week to week, I cringe to think how we would have survived. It did not take me long to realize that Johnny was what I called a "Workaholic." He had a lot of energy and it did not take as much sleep for him as it did for me so I knew this was going to be a huge problem. He had to be doing something all the time, but I felt better if I could grab a nap in the afternoon. I was slowly learning that I needed to pitch in and help with his endeavors.

Johnny did not want me to work away from home because he felt it was his responsibility to be the breadwinner for our family. He said since I could not drive and we only owned the paper wood truck there was no reason for me to look for a job. He firmly believed that it was the husband's job to bring home the bacon and the wife's job was to rear the children. But God had a plan he had not yet revealed to us because He works in mysterious ways that we do not understand. Since I had been a member of First Baptist Church of Robertsdale when Johnny and I met, we continued to attend services there even though we passed right by Johnny's former church, Bethel Baptist, on Sunday mornings on our way to town.

Out of the blue one Sunday night after services in town, Mr. Virgil Buck, my former high school teacher, approached me and offered me a job as his secretary. Mr. Buck became principal of Robertsdale High School in the fall of 1953. Even though I was hesitant because I did not even know how to use a telephone and had never been great at typing, I told him I would like to have the job. I knew we could use the money no matter how small the paycheck. That small salary of $25.00 a week went a long way. Our bills were piling up and we knew that if we could pay a small amount on our furniture and my wedding rings each week, the stores would not repossess the items. I would ride the school bus to and from work. I figured going to work would get me out of the house and maybe I would not have to prove myself to my mother-in-law every day. I was determined to learn to be a good cook. I wanted to make the best coconut pie, banana pudding and fried chicken ever, so people would take note that I was a capable cook. I know now that I was seeking compliments to prove myself; however, that made me try harder to succeed.

I needed a new pair of low heeled shoes to wear to work, so I went to Cooper's Mercantile in town to ask Mrs. Evelyn Cooper if she would let me charge a pair of shoes until I received my first paycheck. She agreed and I kept my word and paid back the $6.00 the following week. Then we drove to Matthew's and Fosberg's Furniture Stores and paid each of them $5.00 on our accounts. We had to charge a kerosene heater from Mr. Fosberg because we had no way to heat the house. Since Mrs. Ryan started supper for us and did some housework I was able to give her $5.00 a week for her needs, too. By Christmas we had paid some bills off and I had saved $50.00 for a shopping trip to

Mobile. We mostly wanted to get Johnny's two nephews, Tommy and Steve, and their little sister, Debbie, a toy each and something for his mother. We were pleasantly surprised when we had enough money left to purchase each other a gift. I chose a pretty plaid pleated wool skirt and he chose a red flannel shirt. Our needs were always met. We were not used to having extra money to spend so we did not miss it. My, how far $50.00 went in 1953. I was glad to be able to help Johnny with a few bills and even though it was not much, it went a long way. It was a happy day when we made the last payment on my wedding and engagement rings.

God was teaching us how to get by on as little as possible and blessing us by keeping us safe. We lived frugally and made a habit of not buying anything else on credit unless it was something we needed very badly. At a Sunday night service at First Baptist a layman named Gerald Coggins, Sr. brought a message on tithing. At the close of the service he asked the couples to stand who would promise the Lord that they would give 10% of their income to the church every payday. Johnny and I both stood at the same time to signify we would. From that day forward no matter how small the income we tithed faithfully and I cannot tell of the ways God has blessed us since we started tithing.

I constantly thought about how dangerous Johnny's job was because we experienced the sadness and disbelief when one of Otto's young brothers was killed in a tragic tractor accident while working in the woods. Without a telephone I sat up late at night wondering when Johnny would get the wood unloaded and make it home. I also did a lot of praying for his safety. Just to prove how young I looked at age eighteen, one night one of the bosses from the mill came to our door and asked me if my daddy was at home. I would always tease Johnny about that and tell him he robbed the cradle when he married me.

I had a lot of hopes and *dreams* for the future. Deep down in my heart, I felt I was capable of accomplishing all the good things in life God had in store for me, no matter that I had a disability that would not go away. I daily battled the handicap that I inherited from Daddy concerning my shaking hands and my low self esteem; I was determined that I would strive to do my best as a wife and mother. I wanted to be a good role model to our children (if God saw fit to bless us with babies). I never stopped *dreaming* that life would get better because I felt without *dreams* there was no hope and my hope for the future was anchored in the Lord.

2
Learning to Drive Stick Shift Trucks

Johnny and his pulpwood truck

I was hesitant about learning to drive the used pick-up truck we managed to purchase after Johnny traded his Ford Convertible for a paper wood truck. However, out of necessity I was put to the test of driving whether I wanted to or not. One Sunday we had lunch with Ruth and Otto. They lived in town and for some reason we had to bring home both the paper wood truck and the pick-up truck. Why both trucks were at their house has slipped my mind, but Johnny told me I would have to drive the pick-up truck home. I had only been in the driver's seat a few times so I was already shaking when I climbed up into the truck. Since I had hardly practiced putting the clutch down with my left foot while shifting into three different gears of low, medium and high I began praying hard that God would be with me and help me make it home safely.

After we turned on Highway 90 and crossed the viaduct that ran over the train tracks, there was not much traffic so I relaxed a bit thinking I was doing pretty well when all of a sudden I felt something run into the back of the truck. As I glanced in my rearview mirror I could see the paper wood truck was pushing me down the highway. What was going on? I had already advised Johnny that I would not drive very fast so why was he pushing me? My first feeling was disbelief and then came the anger. I wondered why he was doing this to me knowing I was just learning to drive much less trying to remember which gear to shift next. My second concern was that there was a danger of our bumpers getting tangled together.

I began to realize that he was carrying out some of his mischievous boyish tricks on me. He was beginning to show me a side of him that I heard about in stories from his relatives. He had never been afraid of anything in his life, but he should have understood that this was my first endeavor to learn to drive by myself. I looked in the mirror again, saw he was laughing, and that made me even madder. As soon as he backed off some I put the pedal to the metal and tried to get as far away from my reckless husband as I could. Once I turned down our lane, I thought I was home-free, but I was wrong. I suddenly realized that I was driving a little too fast as I approached the small four posted carport when I heard both left fenders screech as I scraped the post. I was so mad and frustrated I thought to myself that scratched fenders served him right for making me so nervous on my first solo drive. I began to cry when Johnny explained he was just trying to get me to go faster. I did not intend to ever seek revenge for his misbehavior, but the tables would be turned soon enough.

Early one cold frosty Saturday morning Johnny came back in the house while I was washing the breakfast dishes and said he needed me to drive the paper wood truck to pull off the tractor. Perhaps the cold morning had something to do with the tractor refusing to crank because he had tried several times to get it started but had no luck. So I put on my heavy coat, climbed up in the big wood hauler and rolled my window up while he tied a long chain to the truck. He advised me to take it easy until the chain tightened. I followed instructions and slowly took off up the lane. I perceived I needed to go faster in order for the motor to turn over so I shifted into second and sped up. I never thought to check things out in my rearview mirror; I was so busy trying to figure out if I had the truck in the correct gear. I wondered why Johnny had not called out when the tractor started. At the end of the lane I finally stopped.

When I rolled the window down, Johnny was hollering and fighting mad. He shouted, "What do you mean dragging me up the lane that fast when I was screaming for you to stop because the tractor had started?" He explained that he had almost turned over and had to hold on to the steering wheel for his life as the tractor zigzagged from one side of the road to the other. Above the roar of the engine I had not heard a sound. Remember I had my windows rolled up. I tried to explain to him that I never heard him, but I was just wasting words trying to apologize. It later occurred to me, "What goes around comes around," as I recalled the incident with the pick-up and paper wood trucks. This time the shoe had been on the other foot. I have often wondered if Johnny thought about my scary ride when my life was in his hands. Oh, well, learning to drive a stick shift pick-up truck or an old paper-wood truck was not a priority to me or was it on the top of my list of big *dreams* and accomplishments.

3
Our First Born Son

Proud Papa holding his son, John Barry Ryan, and
Jeanette as new Mama

I had only been working at Robertsdale School for a couple months when we discovered that our first baby was on its way. The due date was early July so I thought I would be able to continue working until school closed for the summer. I never realized I would be so nauseous and my stomach so queasy that I could hardly make myself get up in the mornings and face the day. I knew what it was like to be extremely tired because I had been tired all my life it seemed. However, no one told me this was a normal thing for expectant mothers. I literally forced myself to get out of the warm bed, eat a little oatmeal and dress before the kerosene heater in our chilly bedroom in order to start my short trek up the lane to catch the school bus to my job at school. I would be so sick that I had to stop and heave before I reached my neighbor's house.

I gained very little weight so I was not going to tell anyone about my condition until I could hide it no longer. However, one day I went down to the lunchroom to try to eat something and realized spaghetti was on the menu. Their spaghetti was sometimes greasy and I knew I could not eat it that day. I asked the lunchroom manager, Hattie Fitkin, not to put any spaghetti on my plate and explained that I was not very hungry that day. Hattie, as everyone called her, let out a yell that could be heard all over the lunchroom. She said, "I know what is wrong with you. You're pregnant, aren't you?" My face must have been glowing red because people still did not use the "P" word where children were present. I neither denied nor confirmed her inquisitive question, but the word was out.

A few days later I bundled up to make my daily trip from the office to Central Baldwin Bank in Robertsdale. I carried the money to the bank every day when Mr. Ira Hinote, one of the school bus drivers, went to Daddy Carlson's Garage to fill his bus with gasoline. As I stood by the bank's cashier window still dressed in my heavy winter coat waiting for Vera Lewis to count the money I began to feel faint and clammy. The room was very warm and began to spin around. I told Vera I felt faint and she asked the other cashier, Mr. James Cooper, to help me out the door so the cold air would make me feel better. Sure enough, when the cold air hit my face and I took off my coat I felt much better. Now everyone in the bank knew I was most probably expecting and soon the entire First Baptist Church would know, so I would have to tell my boss, Principal Buck. He probably knew but I kept working and said nothing until one day in March something happened that made me think I would have to resign before I wore maternity clothes to work. The coach's wife, who was expecting and wearing maternity clothes, often came by the office to speak to me. One day she came stomping through the office firing mad because one of the high school boys had made a remark that big bellied teachers needed to stay home. She spoke to Mr. Buck about the situation but I cannot remember what he said.

It was spring and I was gaining weight in the stomach so I knew I did not want some smart-aleck student to talk to me like that. I was too timid to tell Mr. Buck that I would have to quit work so I sent Johnny to his home to tell him. Mrs. Buck approached me later and told me it would be fine to wear maternity clothes to school in order to finish the year. I really wanted to finish the year but I thought it best to resign in April. I was so tired; I thought I should get more rest during the day. I just felt badly leaving Mr. Buck without a secretary that late in the school year. I trained a senior student how to make the deposit and run the menu. It was years before I knew it was a natural thing to be tired.

Back at home I did get to rest more but tried to resume my daily chores since I did not want my mother-in-law to think I was just being lazy. In May, four of Mrs. Ryan's sisters, Emma, Nettie, Mollie and Annie, from North Alabama came to visit. Johnny's mother was very devoted to her five sisters who all lived in nicer homes than our little "cracker box" as Johnny called it. I did not have to worry though because they enjoyed just being together and talked for a long time after they folded down the peach colored couch at bedtime. Aunt Annie stayed with Ruth at night.

I prayed that the mice that had a tendency to wake us up gnawing in the attic would be quiet. But one night a mouse came down from the attic looking for food and started sliding all over the waxed linoleum floor. I heard a big commotion but decided to let the ladies handle the situation. I think the little pest got swatted with the broom. I would wake up when they were having breakfast and discussing events of the past that they could not change but each sister had their own version of the story. I was always hospitable to Johnny's relatives when they visited but it hurt deeply when my mother-in-law whispered to them that I had splurged money when I bought material to sew a dress. I felt I could never measure up to her standards no matter how hard I tried. I showed hospitality to all who came and I fully believe they all liked and respected me. I got to know all of Johnny's relatives and enjoyed their visits. Later on, Johnny's cousin, R. T. Edwards and his wife, Era visited us often. They usually came in the summertime when the peas, butterbeans, tomatoes and okra were ready to pick from the garden and put in the freezer. The four of us would wake up early and go the garden and gather everything. Then we hurried back to the house to prepare a big breakfast before the kids woke up. Their son was Doyle's age and their daughter was Twila's age so they enjoyed each other's company. After breakfast we all got a dishpan and visited while we shelled peas and beans. Then Era and I would cook a very delectable dinner of vegetables from the garden and Southern fried chicken or beef that had been slaughtered and put in the freezer.

On July 3, 1954, we went to Pensacola to visit Johnny's sister, Elsie, and her family. Elsie's husband, Biddle, took Johnny car shopping in downtown Pensacola. He came back with a 1948 Studebaker. I was relieved that we now had dependable transportation since the baby was already overdue. When we arrived home that night, we were very tired and went straight to bed. I awoke the next morning and realized it was time to go to the hospital. We hastily left for Mattie Rhodes Hospital in Bay Minette, Alabama. When we arrived at the hospital we discovered that since it was the fourth of July my doctor was on a fishing trip but his associate, Dr. George Barry Halliday and one nurse was on duty. I would be their only patient that day. I still insisted that my doctor who was celebrating the Fourth of July deliver the baby if he came home from his fishing trip in time. Oh, the foolishness of my immaturity. Dr. Halliday was on duty and I later realized that he was a good family physician who knew what he was doing in the delivery room. I should have requested that he take over.

July 4, 1954 proved to be a very long day for both me and Johnny. Every now and then Dr. Halliday would come into the room to check on me. Late that afternoon the nurse came in and although I was not complaining told Johnny to hold a mask containing gas over my nose so she could do a procedure. I objected to the gas mask and told her I did not need it, but she was adamant and kept giving Johnny orders to hold it over my face although I fought it. A sinking feeling came over me and that was the last thing I remember until some time the next day. Johnny told me that it was nearly midnight when my doctor finally arrived, used his forceps and the baby was born on July 5. According to Johnny the doctor left the hospital while the baby and I were still in the delivery room. I never saw him. I had been sedated for a very long time. Ether was used in those days to keep people asleep, but there were a lot of side effects.

Johnny had a frightening experience when he was waiting in the hallway. The nurse swung open the big delivery room doors, shoved the crying newborn baby, whose head was red from the forceps used during his delivery, into his arms and started running down the hall screaming for Dr. Halliday as she ran. Johnny could see through the big doors that I was deathly sick and was throwing up while still unconscious. He said the doctor tried several different things to bring me around. I did not feel or remember him slapping my face as he tried to revive me. He was telling me that I had something to live for; a new baby boy who needed me. I vaguely heard someone loudly calling my name but I could not move or speak. However the voice in the distance kept getting closer and more demanding as I tried desperately to open my eyes. What I really wanted was to be left alone because I felt no energy to fight to return to the present. I wondered who this person was who would not be quiet and let me slip back into oblivion. However, he never relented until I finally opened my eyes. If not for the determination and perseverance of this good hometown family doctor I probably would not have lived to raise my child. As I lay in the hospital bed the next five days I began to realize that Dr. Halliday had saved my life. I owed him a great deal but had no way to repay him.

I had seen a license plaque from a medical college in the hospital waiting room during prior visits that contained the name George Barry Halliday, M.D. So we named the baby John Barry after his daddy and Dr. Halliday. I stayed in the hospital five days in tremendous pain from the surgical knife and stitches. I was also so weak from the overdose of anesthesia and not eating that I never made it out of bed until I was released. Food tasted so bad I could not eat but a few bites at a time. I was in such bad shape I could not nurse my son so he was constantly crying in the nursery. Every day when Dr. Halliday made his rounds he would stop by and ask me about getting out of bed. I told him I just could not, so he did not press me. The doctor who delivered my baby seemed unconcerned.

The next day, I heard two nurses whisper outside my door that I was the patient they had almost lost. I began to fight to get better because I knew I needed to be able to take care of the baby when I got home. I never stopped hurting during the next two months. After I came home I did not resist when Mrs. Ryan took Barry to bathe, dress or rock him to sleep. She took care of the laundry and washed his diapers and cooked for Johnny. I appreciated the help and she seemed happy to do it, but I eventually had to force myself to get up and do what I could because I wanted my baby to recognize me as his mother. I went back to see my doctor in three weeks and complained about the pain. He said I had a mild infection and advised me what to do. I knew something was terribly wrong because other young mothers did not have as much pain and weakness as I had.

When the baby was only a few weeks old Johnny came home from his National Guard meeting one night and said he and Otto must leave immediately for Georgia on a two week training expedition. I really did not want him to leave since I was still in so much pain, plus suffering from depression that I did not even understand or much less tell Johnny about. When no one was around I would have crying spells. Since Johnny had responsibilities, he made the trip. He had only been gone for a couple of days when everything fell apart. I was taken aback when Mrs. Ryan announced that she needed the car keys one morning. She said she was going to use the car and have Ruth drive her to town. Her domineering attitude upset me terribly. If she had only asked me if she could use the car I do not believe I would have gotten so shook up. I struck back defiantly. I told her she could get Ruth to drive her own car to take her to town because I had the keys to our car and I might need to go to town myself. I thought I should stand up for myself, but the damage was done. I knew I could not take two weeks of her bossing me around so I took the baby and drove to my friend's house in the Bull Springs community and asked if she and her husband would take me to Paxton to visit Daddy and Blannie. They agreed that they could take me.

I went home to pack our clothes. Aunt Bea Rogers who was Mama's sister heard I was not doing well so she brought her daughter, Judy to stay with me for a few days. She thought Judy might be able to help me with the baby. I told them I was going to Daddy's so Aunt Bea said I could take Judy with me to Paxton. When we arrived at Daddy's and Blannie's house, I found Blannie with an infected foot. Since she was a diabetic the doctor had ordered her to stay off her feet. Blannie sat on the long side porch shelling peas Daddy had picked for dinner. I realized my temper and hastiness had really gotten the best of me. I was sick and hurting, had a colicky baby to take care of, and now had the cooking and cleaning to handle. Originally, I thought about staying with them for the summer. I had even thought about never going back home, but now I had a child to think about. I could not work and after giving my friend gas money, I had very little money. But I was determined to make the best of things and would decide later what to do. I knew I needed medical attention but did not know the doctors in Florala or anyone who could take me.

Judy met one of Blannie's nieces that was about her age and they hit it off so she spent a lot of time with her. I cooked and cleaned the kitchen and washed diapers by myself outside on the old ringer washing machine. I had to get up with the baby at night and make my way through the long screened-in back porch to the kitchen in order to heat his bottle as I tried not to wake Daddy and Blannie. As soon as Johnny's unit arrived back home, he got in the car and came after us. I decided I had no choice but to return home even though the relationship may be strained between Johnny's mom and me. I would try to prove myself a capable mother and wife. I loved my baby and nothing would come between us.

I dressed myself and the baby in preparations to go for a six-week check-up but Johnny had to first take his mom to the doctor. She was in pain with her arthritic arm so he did not get back from her doctor appointment in time to take me to mine. It was two months after Barry's birth when I finally went to the doctor again. When I did get to see the doctor who delivered my baby, he came in the room and then went to fetch his nurse who gathered articles on a cart. The doctor performed a procedure to remove the placenta that should have been passed and disposed of when the baby was born. It was pressing on my stitches causing all the pain and preventing them from healing. When I told a friend that the doctor must have been very tired the night of the baby's birth to make such a mistake, she told me it was a miracle I did not get gangrene and die. God's angels must have worked overtime taking care of me during those painful days and months. I immediately felt like a new person after I saw the doctor that Saturday, but resented having to suffer like I did because of his negligence. I was so fortunate Dr. Halliday was on duty that Sunday evening and night as I know he saved my life from the other doctor's negligence. To my regret, I never contacted Dr. Halliday afterwards to thank him for helping me regain consciousness and live to enjoy my baby and the other children I would have.

We never complained to my original doctor but I often wondered if others had been through what I had to bear. It felt so good to be normal again that I tried to forget the whole ordeal. John Barry was growing and healthy although we could not find milk that would agree with him. I was extremely glad to be alive and well. I could now concentrate on my big *dream* of getting indoor plumbing and a new black and white screened television.

4
Taking My Driver's Test

I put off taking my driver's test until after we were able to afford a presentable car. After Barry's birth I knew I needed to learn to drive and get my driver's license. There would be times when Johnny would not be available to drive us to the doctor's office, grocery store or other places. I was apprehensive that I might get a ticket since I was driving without a license while learning. I knew we did not have extra money to pay fines.

I soon picked up a driver's manual and began studying it. One steamy, summer Saturday morning, Johnny drove me into town for my driver's test. When we arrived we found out that I would be the last one to take the test and we would have to wait. Since the weather was hot, six month old Barry got tired and fussy. I was determined to wait it out although I figured I would fail the test because I had not practiced parallel parking. I watched each participant as they returned and parked perfectly between the two cars, received a well done nod from the officer in charge, and left with a smile on their face. Then suddenly, it was my turn. My heart was beating fast as I sat down in the car and my foot shook as I placed it on the accelerator. Then I heard my friend, Hattie Fitkin, whom I had worked with at school, call to the officer as he climbed in beside me. Hattie told him in no uncertain terms that he had better not fail me because I needed my driver's license. It turned out that the Highway Patrolman lived next door to Hattie. I guessed he had been the recipient of some of Hattie's good home cooking since they were neighbors.

As I have often said: the Lord just takes over sometimes when we have such small faith. I was so nervous that I could not think straight. I had no hope of passing the driving test after the trooper told me to turn right and I turned left. Once, I forgot to use my hand signal when I stopped at a stop sign. I knew that mistake did not get me any brownie points. I was dreading the procedure of parallel parking at the end of the test. However, luck was with me, or maybe it was the Lord because when we returned to City Hall, there were no cars remaining. The officer told me to just pull into the parking lot. To my relief, I did not have to parallel park. I knew I had passed the written test, but waited for the final verdict. Having Hattie on my side surely must have been a good thing because I received my license. That day went from hopelessness to celebration. The trooper was probably thinking that he did not want to ride with this lady again or maybe he did not want another tongue lashing from Hattie. I was one jubilant lady that day as I thanked God for working things out for me but knew I still had a lot to learn and a long way to go. Getting my driver's license was a *dream* come true and boosted my confidence and morale that with the help of the Lord I could do whatever I set my mind to do.

5
A Family Thanksgiving Tradition

Thanksgiving at Pop Dyess' cabin in the woods with Uncle Horace and Aunt Ola Shumock, Vivian and Donald Ellers.

After our mother passed away in 1950, Daddy remarried Blannie Bracewell. She was a well educated lady who had been a schoolteacher at one time. I am not sure how Daddy met her but I always suspected it was through the "Lonely Heart's Club". Widows and single people joined the club and the club then matched them up with someone compatible to correspond with. I never put him on the spot and asked him to tell me how they met. After a few visits back and forth they were married in September, 1951, which was one year after Mama died. Blannie had a new 1950 Chevrolet sedan that she drove. She left her furniture and house as it was and moved in with us since Marion and I were still in school. She bought a new dresser for her clothes and they traded bedrooms with

Marion since his was more private. We thought she was there to stay but it was only a temporary thing for her. She knew all along that as soon as we were gone from home she would get Daddy to move back to Paxton, Florida with her. She was anxious to get back to her old community where two of her sisters and her brother lived.

My three brothers and I never thought much about beginning a wonderful Thanksgiving tradition the first year we gathered at our stepmother's big house near the state line of Florida and Alabama. They decided to celebrate this holiday in Paxton, Florida so the men could hunt and Blannie could visit with her relatives. I was dating Johnny so I invited him to come. My older brother, Ernest, brought a young woman by the name of Vivian with him. Vivian and I shared a bedroom and Johnny and Ernest bunked together. My brother, Marion, also went with us for Thanksgiving. Bernard was in Germany at the time.

The big house had been built by Blannie's parents. After their deaths, Blannie and her first husband bought it. Blannie took a ham to cook along with the sweet potatoes and other vegetables. She made a plain cake with coffee icing that was really good for dessert. We enjoyed our meal together on Thursday in the big dining room. I admired her lovely antique dishes and china in her china cabinet that we used for setting the table and serving the food. Blannie never seemed to be concerned that someone would break in and steal it with her away from her home. We went to drive-in theatres on Friday and Saturday nights. The men enjoyed quail hunting for a couple of days and we fried the quail for lunch on Saturday. After lunch on Sunday we took some pictures in the front yard by the camellia bushes and then returned to our homes. These yearly festive celebrations of the Dyess clan became such an enjoyable family time together. The only thing that would keep us home on Thanksgiving after that first year was an illness in the family.

The house had large rooms with three fireplaces and an iron cook stove in the kitchen that was fired up in the winter to warm us while we cooked. Although we used the oven of the old wood stove to bake sweet potatoes and sometimes biscuits, we mostly used the electric stove to cook on. One fireplace was located in the living room, one in the room where Daddy and Blannie slept, and one in a back bedroom. No matter how hard we tried, Johnny and I never arrived in time to acquire the privilege of claiming the back bedroom. As soon as school was out, Ernest and Rachel headed that way and he always had a blazing fire in the fireplace warming the room when we arrived. On cold mornings we dressed very quickly and ran to warm at the nearest fireplace or kitchen stove because it always seemed to freeze on Thanksgiving Day.

The next summer after I married, Marion dropped out of school to work. I was stunned when Daddy and Blannie came over to our house and asked me to sign papers so he could sell our old home place. Daddy who had worked as a butcher for so many years at Hinote Packing Company suddenly quit his job. They told me that they planned to move to Blannie's home in Paxton during the summer of 1953. I was sorrowful that Daddy was selling our red roof house in the Bull Springs Community. He was breaking ties with our old neighbors and friends and relatives in Baldwin County which had been his home since birth. There was much work to be done at Blannie's home place since it had remained unoccupied for a year or two so Daddy and Marion begin cleaning the area around the house, planting a garden and repairing fences. Marion moved with them, but Bernard was still in the Army in Germany and Ernest had settled in Perry County where he taught school. They had no idea Daddy was selling the house Ernest and Bernard had helped him restore. I was the only one left in Baldwin County. Even though I felt somewhat abandoned by my family, this was my home and I never intended to leave the area.

Bernard, soon returned from Germany, received his discharge from the Army and settled down with Daddy and Blannie. He met Ethel Hoover at church and they planned to be married as soon as she graduated from high school. However, they married during her Christmas break from school because Bernard got a chance to purchase a house and farm near Daddy but could not secure a loan unless he was married. Ethel returned to school and graduated in the spring.

The men really looked forward to hunting quail in the woods and swamps. They all began to bring their smelly, barking birddogs along. Sometimes the dogs barked at the other strange dogs during the night so no one received much shut-eye, but we were up before dawn on Thanksgiving Day. After the women prepared breakfast, the men were off for an exciting hunt. Sometimes they would kill up to 50 or 60 quail and dress them for our dinner for the next two days. When the dogs sniffed a covey of quail they stopped immediately in their tracks and pointed to alert the hunters. Their tails would point straight out and sometime one foot would be pulled up if they were running. Old Joe would freeze in his position until ordered to flush the birds so Johnny could fire at them as they retreated in the sky. Johnny and my brothers had been good sharp shooters in the service and they were good at bringing down the bird they aimed for, sometimes more than one at a time. The flutter and sound of quail being flushed from hiding places could startle a hunter. But the adrenalin flowed and the shots sounded out. The dogs would not retrieve the birds until their owner's gave orders. It was quite a thrill for the men to see the dogs bring the quail to their masters. The dogs only obeyed the person who had trained them. Around the dinner table there was much discussion concerning which dog got the prize for its outstanding performance or why someone's dog acted hastily.

We started frying quail early on Friday morning because it took some time to fill platters of fat juicy birds. If you have never tasted this delicacy, you cannot imagine how delicious they were served with rice, brown gravy and hot biscuits. Just thinking about this delicacy makes my taste buds go wild.

When we gathered for Thanksgiving of 1953, both Rachel and I were expecting. The babies would be born just a few months apart. I never figured out why Rachel did not have morning sickness when she got up in the morning. I had such nausea that I could not stand to smell the odors of bacon frying, coffee brewing or anything else cooking. When I went to the kitchen to try to help out I would have to leave, so when it was time to prepare the meals during Thanksgiving weekend, Rachel helped Blannie cook and I washed dishes later that afternoon after lunch when I felt better. No matter what I tried to eat it would not stay down but I was happy just being with my brothers, their wives, and Daddy and Blannie. I could *dream* of the day when food would once again taste and smell good and I could enjoy eating after my baby was born.

Times were hard for us during the nineteen fifties. Four years after they moved back to her home Blannie suffered a brain aneurism in September of 1956. Bernard called Uncle Ted Cooper at his store in Rosinton and he drove over to tell me Daddy wanted me to come. Johnny drove me to Paxton, but by the time I got there Blannie had already lapsed into a coma. I talked to her and read the 23rd Psalm out loud as I sat by her bed. I had hoped I would get there in time to talk to her about the Lord. I had never questioned her about her salvation although I knew she occasionally attended church. Now I pondered whether or not she had asked Jesus to come into her heart and had given her life to Him. Now my window of opportunity had passed. I realized that she only had a couple of days left on this earth because as she breathed I could hear the death rattles. She and Daddy had only been married five years. Blannie's funeral was held at her home in the large living room. Some people sat in rocking chairs on the front porch. Johnny came up for the funeral and brought Barry. His mother kept him while I was sitting with Blannie and helping out. Ethel had been there washing bed clothes and lifting Blannie even though she was expecting her first child. Blannie's will stated that Daddy could stay in the house as long as he lived, but at his death it would return to her sisters and brothers. While Daddy was gone to read the will Blannie's relatives came to claim all of her antique dishes, her best quilts and other items. I never said a word, but thought they should have waited until Daddy got back. Daddy would stay in the big house only as long as he had to.

Daddy was very lonesome and grief stricken so when November came Daddy wrote me that he still wanted all of us to come up for Thanksgiving as we had done before. When we all arrived on Wednesday night we found out Ethel was not well. That night before we went to bed Ethel told me she thought she was about to lose her baby. I was with her when she miscarried and I went to tell Bernard to take her to the hospital. Our holiday was turning out to be a sad one since we would be missing Blannie, Bernard, Ethel and Marion, who was away in the Marines. That year the rest of us gathered together but had not put much thought into our Thanksgiving meal. We were all barely making ends meet and money for food was scarce, but luckily Johnny had killed two wild Mallard ducks at Bull Springs Creek that we dressed, iced down and carried with us. When we arrived at Daddy's we found out that Bernard had also shot a couple of ducks that day. Rachel and I cooked the ducks and made dressing for our Thanksgiving dinner. We made the dressing the way Blannie had taught us. She always made the best dressing. We watched her, took note of the ingredients, and used her recipe for future Thanksgiving dinners. The meal was not elaborate that year but when one cannot afford turkey or ham, duck tastes pretty good. The Lord had provided and on the morrow we would partake of our special meal of quail that only hunters or maybe the "Children of Israel" *dreamed* of dining on.

6
The Sagebrush Fire

Johnny's Bird dog's with Joe in front pointing quail in the sage grass.
Queen and Checker are backing up

When Thanksgiving rolled around in 1954, Ernest and Rachel had become the proud parents of Steven Forrest and Johnny and I had welcomed John Barry into our lives. We had not been able to visit since the babies were born so I could hardly wait for Thanksgiving to come. We planned to leave for Daddy's that afternoon as soon as Johnny got home from work, ate a bite and loaded our things. I hurriedly packed our suitcases and cleaned the house that Wednesday. I never wanted to return to a dirty house. Johnny and I had established one habit that was not good and that was the way we burned our trash. Johnny put a big barrel in the back yard away from the house so we could burn our garbage. I noticed it was pretty windy when I poured the garbage in the barrel and lit the match, but I intended to watch it until most of it was disintegrated, however as I watched I heard Barry crying from his crib. He had wakened from his nap early.

I decided to just step in the house to let him know I had not deserted him. It only took me a minute or two to change his diaper before I hurriedly returned to watch the fire. My heart skipped a beat the moment I stepped into the back yard. With one look I realized I was in serious trouble. It appeared that some paper had blown from the trash can that left a charred trail of burned grass that traveled straight eastward to our neighbor's 40 acre field of tall sage grass. Just as I reached for the water hose, I saw the fire ignite the dry grass and the flames billow upward. The hose would not reach that far and the swift wind was spreading the fire fast. No one in my neighborhood had a telephone and in those days our community of Elsanor did not have a fire department. I realized the fire was out of control and that I could do nothing to put it out. I had an overpowering feeling of panic and helplessness. What was I going to do? Johnny had taken the car to work so I had no way to go for help; plus I had to take care of my crying baby. What if the fire reached Mr. and Mrs. Siebert's house? I feared for Mrs. Siebert's life because she was getting older and could not move very fast.

I ran into the house, grabbed Barry and a bottle of milk, wrapped him tightly and slammed the door behind me. I ran as fast as I could up the smoke filled lane toward my next door neighbor, Eleanor "Runt" Cooper's house. When I reached the dirt road I saw a black pick-up truck rounding the corner. I flagged down my neighbor, Ellis Spivey, and told him the field was burning and I was afraid for Mrs. Siebert and her house. He told me that he would go home pick up his wife, Yvonne, and then get Mitt and Mildred Davis who ran a nearby dairy to help fight the fire. I felt helpless as I paced Mrs. Cooper's yard. She tried to console me by saying the field needed burning, but I was still worried wondering what damage the fire would do. I was afraid someone would get injured fighting it or that the house would burn down.

Before long, I saw a big dozer from the forestry department plowing fire lanes around the entire field. After the fire subsided Ellis returned and informed me that they had saved the Siebert house by dipping corn sacks in water and fighting the fire back as it approached it, but the corn crib was gone. Ellis told me to go back home and take care of the baby. I went back down the lane with a worried countenance only to find out that the inside lock on the back door had not been turned off and I had locked myself out. I had to lay Barry on the cold ground and climb in a bedroom window so we could get inside. As I took care of the baby's needs I wondered how much we would owe for the corn and corncrib that burned. I waited for Mr. Hardy who was the forest ranger who saw the fire from the fire tower near Seminole to arrive. Every day he climbed up the high tower and kept an eye out for fires in all directions. He could see for miles so when he saw the smoke from the burning field he loaded up the dozer and hurried to the scene. When he knocked on the door and asked me if I had caused the fire, I admitted I had let it get away from me. I knew all along that I would tell the truth because I had been taught not to lie when I was a child. I would have looked pretty foolish since he had seen the yard if I had not admitted it was my fault when it was so obvious.

Although I was dreading confronting Johnny I knew he would somehow pay what we owed. I had learned a very valuable lesson concerning burning trash on windy days. Mr. Hardy handed me a ticket for the state's expenses and told me to tell Johnny to go see Mr. Siebert and settle up with him after he got home from work. We had to pay $40.00 for the loss of the Siebert's corn crib but I cannot remember how much the Forestry Department charged us. I wondered how we were going to be able to pay all this, but I was relieved when he told me that Mrs. Siebert was not injured only shook up. That night I thanked God for his help and for caring neighbors. Things could have been so much worse. The Seibert's house could have burned if not for concerned neighbors who became involved.

We did make it to Daddy's and Blannie's that Thanksgiving night and enjoyed being together. After we had our Thanksgiving dinner and the men left for the evening hunt Rachel and I built a big fire in the living room and put a quilt on the floor to watch our babies play while we visited. In our haste to leave on Wednesday night Johnny mistakenly failed to pick up the bag with Barry's sleepers and other clothes in it so I had to borrow baby clothes from Rachel and keep them washed. Thank goodness he got the bag with the cloth diapers.

I never bought a throwaway diaper but used cloth diapers when the children came along. All my friends used cloth diapers, too. I am not sure why, but it seemed that the weather was always cold during Thanksgiving in those days. There was a bathroom between two of the bedrooms but no hot water heater or space heater, so we did not linger long in there during cold weather. The kitchen was always the warmest place to be because Daddy always had a big box of stove wood in the corner of the kitchen. He would build a fire in the iron stove to warm the room and heat water for washing dishes. If we had sweet potatoes we baked them in the big cook stove. We mostly cooked on the electric stove and ate at a big kitchen table so the large kitchen kept us cozy. The dining room was practically abandoned when the weather was so cold.

A family tradition was started in that big house on the hill that would last for years to come. Of course, once in awhile there would be discussions concerning who would hunt where or who killed the most quail but those were the best of times just spending quality family time together. I thank God for the memories I hold in my heart of those long ago days when we were all together whether it was in the spacious white clapboard house with the sprawling front and side porches or the little house with only one fireplace Daddy built in the woods. We were a family no matter where we met and that said it all.

After Blannies' death Daddy soon married again for the third time. He never learned to cook and keep house so he really needed a helpmate. We all liked Miss Lillie Story because she was a hard worker and was glad to see us when we visited. Her only son abandoned her and stopped sending her a check from the Army after she wrote him she married. She never told us why, if she did know why. We became her family and we were happy that she was taking care of Daddy. She could make the best big biscuits but she never let them brown on top. Johnny would beg her to burn him a biscuit. Once they accidently browned too much and she called out, "Oh my goodness, I've got Johnny Ryan biscuits." As to the many bird dogs that made the trip to Paxton, Florida to hunt quail there were several, but I think Johnny's favorite dog was old Joe. Johnny was working on a TDY trip at Eglin Field near Ft. Walton one year so he took old Joe up to Daddy's to stay during the week so he could drive over for the weekend to hunt with him. Daddy was supposed to keep Joe tied but he never did like the idea of a dog not having its freedom so he let him run loose. Joe stayed close by the house because he knew that Miss Lillie would throw him a biscuit after breakfast every morning.

Joe had faced the challenge of wrestling with snakes by shaking them and breaking their necks until they died, but one day Joe got in a situation bigger than he could handle. On that day there were small children visiting Daddy and Miss Lillie. As they played in the front yard a big rattlesnake crawled out of the woods. The children saw it and started screaming "Snake, Snake." Joe rushed over and grabbed the snake by its body and began shaking it in order to break its neck. However, the snake was approximately eight feet long with a large body and was too big for Joe to handle. Daddy quickly grabbed his gun and shot the snake. He and Joe walked a little way in the woods to dispose of the snake and then Daddy drove over to warn Bernard to watch out for the rattlers because they were crawling and they were big. When Daddy returned he found Old Joe dead under the steps. Joe's head was swollen because he had on a collar and it choked him to death. With that much venom in him there would have been no way he could have lived. Daddy did not know that the big rattler had bitten Johnny's favorite dog.

Daddy was so upset and worried about how he was going to tell Johnny about old Joe. Since he had no way of getting in touch with Johnny he had to wait until he got there on Friday night. Johnny came in and Daddy told him what had happened. He was sad to lose his best birddog, but relieved the children and Daddy had not been bitten. After their talk Miss Lillie called them to supper and they sat down to eat. When Johnny finished Miss Lillie asked him how he liked the hash she cooked. He told her it was good to which she broke out in a big laugh. Johnny looked at her and said, "Miss Lillie, did you feed me coon hash?" Miss Lillie never confirmed whether it was coon hash or not but he knew because her laugh gave it away.

There would be other dogs to train to point birds. Johnny still had Joe's offspring, Queen, Spec and Checker, to point the quail and carry on the job of bringing him enough birds to fill his hunting jacket. So Daddy's marriage to Miss Lillie did not break our Thanksgiving tradition of gathering together. We fondly remember our early visits with Blannie and Daddy and later with Daddy and Miss Lillie. We would carry on as a family as long as the Lord permitted. Families are forever if we hold our loved ones and *dreams* in our hearts.

7
Cars of Days Gone By

1939 Mercury and Nephews

The Hudson Commodore

1948 Ford Convertible

1951 Studebaker Champion with 1940 LaSalle in back

Our first new car a 1956 Pontiac Catalina

the 1989 Cadillac Brougham that John was so proud to own later in life

8
Decoration Day

The seven Edwards siblings met in their Sunday finery to place flowers on relative's graves at Hopewell Cemetery and to later attend a family reunion at sister-in-law Annie Edward's home in Hanceville, AL. Front: Maggie Nichols, Emma McMurray, Annie Benton, and Mamie Ryan. Back: Nettie Self, Jerry Edwards and Mollie Lake

After making the trip home from Castle AFB in California, my new friend, John, traded his prized 1939 green Mercury Cavalier to Howard Vaughn of Elsanor for a paper wood truck. He later invested in an exquisite old Hudson car that had been a classic in its day, but he did not keep it very long. John picked me up for church services one Sunday night and left me at my front door afterward. I went in, dressed for bed and went to sleep never knowing that the Hudson had not started. He had to sleep in the car for several hours until the motor cooled and it would crank. I know his mother was worried about him that night and wondered why he had stayed out so late. He later got a chance to purchase a 1948 Ford convertible hot rod that he drove until after we married. We made a lot of trips to Pensacola, Mobile, Gulf Shores and to the Fairhope pier with the top down. Not wanting my hair to blow in the wind, I always wore a silk bandana scarf that was stylish and very colorful.

One Saturday night shortly after our first date, John was supposed to pick me up at 7:00 pm but as I watched the clock, I began to think he had stood me up. When he knocked on the door, I went outside because I wanted to hear his excuse for being so late. He explained that he had his mother in the car. I thought to myself, "Why do we need a chaperone just to go bowling." John quickly explained that he and his mother had been on a long trip to Hanceville, Alabama, to attend his Uncle Jerry Edward's funeral. He said he had driven the Ford hard trying to get back in time. He apologized for not letting me know he would be late but said he had no means of communication. Neither of us had telephones. They departed early that morning before dawn so he could not tell me about the emergency trip. Those were the days when there were no interstates so it took much longer to get to North Alabama. I understood when he explained the situation and told him we could go bowling another time, but he said if I would go out with him he would take his mother home first. I realized later that since he was responsible for taking care of his mother after his dad died, that there would be many times she would accompany us when we went to visit their relatives and to other places.

The summer I turned 17, Johnny invited me to go with him and other family members to North Alabama in May of 1951 to attend "Third Sunday Decoration Day" at the cemetery where his dad and many other relatives were laid to rest. I declined because I did not have a proper Sunday dress to wear. I had heard that his mother saved all year in order to purchase a new outfit complete with hat and gloves. Since Johnny was in the Air Force stationed at Brookley Field he had a small income so he offered to take me shopping for a new dress. I thought that would not be appropriate and declined his offer at first, but he continued to urge me to shop for a dress. I knew if Mama had not died she could have made me a dress as stylish as could be purchased in a store. If, I went to meet his relatives I wanted to look presentable. I finally relented and we went to Mobile where I found a reasonably priced pink waffle pique sundress with a jacket that could be left open or buttoned up the front. I was excited to have a dress that I could wear on special occasions, but still felt that people would talk about Johnny buying my clothes if they found out.

We left home at dark on a Friday night with Johnny, his mother, me and one of his nephews in the Ford. Following along behind were, Otto, Ruth and their youngest son. Otto drove a big truck loaded with watermelons to sell in Cullman when we arrived there on Saturday. Of all the things to happen the big truck ran out of gas that night in the middle of nowhere. Back then all of the gas stations closed during the night and would not open until morning so we tried to doze in the vehicles until daybreak. On Saturday we got acquainted with the relatives in Hanceville and spent the night with Johnny's Aunt Nettie. Around ten o'clock on Sunday morning all the relatives met at the cemetery to decorate the graves. Mrs. Ryan picked flowers from her yard to take and they had purchased several dozen gladiolas to decorate with. I noticed all the graves had fresh flowers on them as my eyes scanned the huge cemetery. It was a beautiful sight to behold. Artificial flowers had not been thought of in 1951, but the fresh flowers were gorgeous. There was a large cedar tree that we all huddled under in order to stay out of the hot sun. Other relatives seeking shade would stop by and I was introduced to dozens of cousins, aunts and uncles. The big Edwards reunion at his Aunt Annie Edward's home was the highlight of the trip.

We spent two nights while there. On Sunday afternoon we drove to Birmingham to stay with Johnny's Aunt Emma and her husband. They must have been well off because they lived in a nice two-story home in a good neighborhood. When bedtime came, Johnny slept downstairs and I went upstairs to sleep in a large room with Mrs. Ryan and his Aunt Emma. It had been their children's room when they were growing up. They talked a long time after we went to bed and then they both fell asleep and started snoring. I got very little sleep that weekend because I was not accustomed to hearing the room enveloped with such snoring and snorting. I did enjoy meeting his cousins with whom we formed close relationships. Johnny sold the Ford hotrod convertible after we married and he began driving the pulpwood trucks. He took the car to Daddy Carlson's Garage in town and put a "For Sale" sign on it. A guy who wanted a fast running car bought it.

He was struggling trying to make a living in the pulpwood industry. He did not make enough profit to pay our bills with such huge expenses from owning and operating two paper wood trucks. One Saturday we were riding down the narrow dirt road that led from our lane to the fork where it dead ended at Black-Water Creek. We had to pull over to let a man pass that Johnny knew. Mr. Allen stopped to speak to us. He owned land down the road and somehow Johnny knew that he was a union boss who was connected with DuPont Construction. We heard that DuPont Construction Company was building the new Chemstrand plant in Cantonment, Florida. Johnny asked him if he thought he could get a job as a construction worker at the site. Mr. Allen told him to be at his union office in Mobile early Monday morning and ask for him. When Johnny arrived at Mr. Allen's office he was hired on the spot and told to go straight to work at the plant in Pensacola. His salary would be about $90.00 a week which was good pay in those days.

Now that he had another job he had to sell the paper wood trucks. I was so relieved that Johnny would not be working in the woods anymore because it was such a dangerous and tiresome job. In dire need of transportation back and forth to work, he then bought a 1940 La Salle car that had been a gorgeous classic luxurious car in its day. It was a short notch better than the Cadillac. The car offered terrific styling with its signature grill flanked by 2 mounted headlights that protruded from the sides of the hood. It reminded me of some of the luxury cars that belonged to the gangster mobs of the prohibition days that I saw in the movies. It was big; it was black; it was exquisite; but the 1940 LaSalle was then 13 years old and had a lot of wear and tear on it and high mileage.

He drove it to work, to church and to the movie theatre in town. During the winter months our pastime was driving to the old theatre in town even though we hardly ever knew what was playing. The Robertsdale theatre had a calling card to get people to come to the movies in 1953. When you entered the foyer of the old theatre they took your picture when you purchased a ticket and if your picture appeared on the screen when you were watching the movie, you were the lucky winner of whatever the jackpot for the night was. One night Johnny's mother thought it might just be her lucky night and asked us to take her to the movies. I doubted she would win anything, but sure enough during the movie there was her picture right there on the screen. She was overwhelmed and excited to receive the prize money because she did not have a job. That was the good news of the night because when the movie was over the old LaSalle refused to crank.

I was so embarrassed when I had to get behind the wheel and try to start it while Johnny and some boys pushed it off. It made me not want to go to the movie theatre again. We also enjoyed visiting relatives for Sunday dinner and attending Saturday night church socials with our friends from Bethel. If we were not at Johnny's sister, Elsie's and her husband, Biddle's, for Sunday dinner, we were at Ruth and Otto's, or they came to have lunch with us. We always carried Mrs. Ryan along with us so she could spend time with her grandchildren.

That summer our pastor and his wife came to visit us one evening and I asked them to stay for supper not realizing I did not have any meat to cook. So while they visited with Johnny's mother I got in the old LaSalle and took off for Lon Cooper's General Store to buy pork chops. Just as I turned onto busy Highway 90, the motor died. I was afraid I was going to be hit as I sat there in the middle of the road but my guardian angel soon sent two men I knew to stop behind me and offer to give the car a push. Luckily it started so I continued on only to find out that when I turned into the store parking lot I had no brakes. The car flew past the gas pumps barely missing them and several parked cars. I was frantic as to what to do before it came to me to turn off the key. After I did this the car miraculously stopped. I was shaking like a leaf when I went into the store and tried to figure out which cuts of meat was the cheapest because I knew I was going to have to charge it and we usually just charged the basic grocery items. By the time Johnny got home supper was ready and he was surprised to see we had meat instead of the usual dried beans. I should not have been driving without a license so I shudder to think what might have happened if I had ran into someone else's vehicle.

Shortly after that day on a rainy Saturday we needed to pay our taxes at the court house in Bay Minette and Johnny insisted that I get in some driving practice. I promised myself I would never drive that monster of a car again, but he insisted. It seems that the court house stayed open until noon on Saturdays. So after we passed Loxley, Johnny kept urging me to drive a little faster. I was not familiar with the big ultra heavy car and did not like to go the speed limit. I should not have been driving fast because he had forewarned me the tires were almost threadbare and if I heard a loud noise, to get on the brakes. That really made me nervous. As I rounded a curve a strange feeling came over me that something was going to happen and I let off on the gas and said a prayer for safety.

We were not too far from Stapleton when all of a sudden I heard a loud bang that sounded like a shot gun blast. I immediately panicked, slammed on the brakes, and suddenly lost all control of the steering wheel. We were spinning out of control. Johnny grabbed the steering wheel and fought frantically with all his might as he tried to get control of the car. I screamed and prayed in fear. I really needed my guardian angel. The big car rocked back and forth from the right side of the road to the left, then back to the center with tires screeching the entire time. We thought it would turn over any minute so I braced as much as I could readying myself for the crash. Johnny let go of the wheel and wrapped his arms around me. We turned the wheel loose and rode in the ditch for sometime when finally it tried to climb a bank. That stopped the car. Fortunately there was not a lot of traffic on the road that day. It had begun to rain, so we just sat in the car shaking, thanking God that we were not injured and that He had protected us. We realized the car was facing south headed back the way we had come. In a short time a Good Samaritan in a truck came by and offered to pull us out of the ditch and help Johnny change the tire. Most strangers never passed people by who needed help in the fifties, but came to their aid always refusing any pay. We finally made it home and I decided I would wait until we got a better car before I would get behind the wheel again. Driving put too much stress on my guardian angel and me. Johnny took it all in stride but I realized without God's protection we could have been in a terrible accident.

Sometimes later the LaSalle's motor needed repairing so Johnny worked on it whenever he was off work. For the first time we were stranded without transportation. Johnny rode to work at DuPont with a group of men who picked him up at the highway, but he had to walk the mile to meet them. As a last resort we had to move in with Elsie and Biddle and their family of six who lived in Pensacola. After Elsie got Biddle off to work she would drive Johnny to work and then pick him up after work. We felt we were really imposing on them since we slept in the girl's bedroom. That is when Johnny got real serious about car shopping. The repair parts for the LaSalle were so expensive and he decided the old car was ready to be retired to the junk yard. We came home and opened the mail and rejoiced that Johnny had received notice that Brookley Air Force Base was hiring aircraft mechanics. He was offered a job at Brookley Air Force Base with a starting salary of $1.60 an hour plus insurance. Even though it would mean less pay per week he decided to take the job because he knew this job would be more permanent.

Today as we reflect on the old vehicles of the past, we hold fond memories of the different modes of transportation we owned. Our vehicles usually carried us where we needed to go but we often searched for more reliable and dependable means of travel. Johnny determined that he would work hard and someday own a new car that he could depend on to crank and not break down on the road. He secretly *dreamed* that there just might be a nice luxurious Cadillac in the distant future, but he would make no mention of that to me for years to come. For the time being he just needed a vehicle that would take him to work and his family where we needed to go. He found that in the Studebaker. We left the LaSalle at his sister and brother-in-law's Gilbert and Mary Lawton's house in Pensacola and later traded it for a boat. We never looked back.

9
Old Cars Never Die

~~~~~~~~~~~

The following poem was written by my brother, George Marion Dyess. The words came to him after he bought and restored a 1956 Bel-Air Chevrolet car.

Walking through a junk yard watching them crush old cars one day,
A man he came running and shouting! Don't treat that old car that way.
I know she doesn't look so well, but she's got a great story to tell.
Let me buy her from you, I'll restore her like new one day.
It will never again be in your way. Old cars they will never die.

Old cars, I see them as they go passing by
With their coats of shinning armor
Yes, I sometimes see them in the sales lots, where the prices are so high,
And often in a junk graveyard near where their original master lies,
Old cars, they will never, never die.

Old cars, if they could talk, what stories they could tell,
Of sweethearts on dates and love words spoken to a future mate
Of Marriage proposals and a gold wedding band.
Old cars, they were the greatest, the greatest in the land.
Old cars, they will never, never die.

Old cars, cruising down the highways in a parade:
You can hear their engines whine.
And in them their owners sit holding their heads high,
They go to a car show, hoping they will win first prize.
Old cars, they will never, never die.

Old cars, upon the auction blocks they sit,
You can hear the auctioneer roar,
Who will give me 30, 40, 50,000 or more?
Old cars, no longer are they owned by the poor.
Old cars, they will never, never die.

By: George M. Dyess

10
First Adventures in Farming

Watermelons ready to load in 18 wheeler

Turkeys Johnny hatched

Hogs we raised for meat and to sell

Cattle grazing in lush winter pasture

A City Boy Turned Country

In 1960, our oldest son, Barry enrolled in the first grade at Elsanor School. Johnny stopped traveling to other cities on TDY trips to different Air Force bases and we began planting a few small crops. As I said when we married we only owned ten acres of land, but eventually purchased an adjoining twenty acres. We had not been married long when we cleared some of the land by the house and decided to get Mr. Johns to plant corn for us so we could have it ground into feed for our milk cow and the few hogs we were raising. When it came time to pick the corn, a wind had blown the stalks over. Johnny hooked up a trailer to the 1956 Pontiac and drove it slowly down the rows so we could pull the corn from the stalks and throw the ears in the trailer. I knew we had to harvest the corn, but I prayed the car doors would not get too many scratches on them.

In the meantime someone loaned John an old incubator. Since he had raised and flown homing pigeons as a boy, he was so anxious to try his luck at raising turkeys, quail, peacocks and chickens. He was faithful to turn the eggs every day and hatched quite a variety of birds. I had never cooked a pheasant, but found they were a delicacy when baked with dressing, when he finally let me cook one. Of course, I suppose our favorite game was quail but Johnny mostly used them to train his bird dogs. He did not want to kill the turkeys that he managed to raise. One day the hen turkey had the baby turkeys out in the pasture and a rain shower came up. The tiny birds turned their beaks up toward the sky and drowned. I was at home but did not realize this would happen. Another evening Johnny came upon one of our neighbors who had moved behind us. He had spied our tame turkeys roaming the back ten acres and decided he would have roast turkey for dinner. Johnny caught him with his gun aimed at a turkey and halted his hunting expedition. He had already shot two of the tame birds. Johnny gave him a chance to pay for them or he would report him to the game warden. The man paid for the turkeys and we were never bothered with him again. When Mr. Johns bought a new tractor and sold us his smaller Massy Ferguson tractor, Johnny was now ready to start farming.

The next year our project was sweet potatoes. We planted a small patch near the swamp. Johnny purchased an old Irish potato digger that he converted to dig the sweet potatoes. I gathered the round bushel baskets and began to pick up the sweet potatoes as Johnny started digging. I knew this was going to be a tough job since I had picked up Irish potatoes as a teenager and they were much smaller. Boy! Those taters had grown so big, they split open. Yes, picking up Irish potatoes was a hard job, but I soon found out I could hardly drag the basket of sweet potatoes when it was only half full. It was a backbreaking job but I knew Johnny needed my help and we needed the extra money to supplement his salary.

We were both relieved when we finished digging our crop of sweet potatoes and hauled them to the back yard. Now it was time to fill large barrels of water and begin washing the dirty sweet potatoes so we could peddle them. Johnny knew of a settlement of black people in Pensacola who always looked for peddlers of greens, sweet potatoes and other fresh vegetables. They even asked him to bring them coons, opossums and rabbits. While John was at work his mother and I washed the potatoes and sorted out the large cracked ones. On Saturdays he took a load of sweet potatoes to Pensacola to sell, but those he could not sell he gave to Elsanor School's lunchroom manager, Mrs. Eva Ducheneau, to cook for the students. Mrs. Eva used whatever the local farmers brought her, so she made sweet potato pie, candied sweet potatoes, baked sweet potatoes, fried sweet potatoes and every other way she could think of preparing them. Then one day Barry came home from school and said, "Daddy please do not give Miss Eva any more sweet potatoes. We are sick of having to eat sweet potatoes every day." Poor kid, I also cooked them, but I do not remember making him eat them at home.

The following year Johnny and Otto, decided they would clear up a spot of new ground on the ten acres near the house and plant a crop of cucumbers and okra. I was really worried when they said they first would have to dynamite a water hole by the swamp in case they needed to water the cukes. When the vegetables were ready to be picked, Ruth helped the men while I kept the kids and started supper. At that time Barry and Doyle were still small and so were our nieces, Debbie and Olivia. I was pretty frazzled trying to keep the kids busy playing and satisfied and prepare supper for all of us at the same time. I wondered if growing cucumbers was worth all the hard work.

We were learning to farm from trial and error. But one Saturday evening we really could have used some advice. I had my heart set on attending my tenth year Robertsdale High School reunion that Saturday night since I had missed the fifth one, but Johnny said he needed to get the soy bean seed in the ground and could use my help. So, I was a disgruntled wife that afternoon as I sat on the back of the old pick-up and waited to load the hoppers with seed. I never could adjust to all work and no play, but I played the role of the help mate and obedient wife. We finished the job by dark and went back to the house where Johnny's mother was keeping the boys. A few days later we went down to see if the beans had come up. Much to our dismay the seed died because Johnny had adjusted the planter to 36 inch rows, but forgot to adjust the fertilizer hopper. The seed went on top of the fertilizer and killed the germination. We later had to replant, and I always thought if we had taken the afternoon off and gone to the class reunion things might have turned out differently.

A few years later, we got a chance to buy forty acres of land for $100.00 an acre on the winding sandy road that joined our other property. It sure did not look like much because it had become the community dump. The people who owned it lived out of state and had never seen the property they inherited. The land was completely covered with weeds and oak samplings and garbage. Garbage such as tin cans, broken glass and old paper was strewn everywhere. I could not foresee that it would be an appropriate site for our future home. We hired a man who owned a bull dozer and he soon started clearing the land. He found a big cattle-dipping vat buried deep in the ground on one corner of the property. It took a lot of work to extract a tall tree and dig a hole to bury the vat. No one thought of preserving history in those days. After the garbage had been put into piles with the brush and burned, it took a long time to pick up the broken glass strewn everywhere.

Johnny saw the newly plowed ground as a field of vine ripe watermelons while I saw it as a jungle of scrub oaks, broken bottles and rotten garbage. But we both visualized the property as a nice home site when the land was cleared. There was a big live oak tree near the property line on one side not far from the road so we decided that would be a good spot to build our house. By the time spring arrived the land was cleared, the stumps pushed up and burned and the seed planted in the new ground. Daddy came down to teach Johnny how to plant the watermelon seed since he had never grown them before. Daddy had planted a lot of watermelons during his lifetime. He was what we now call a Master Gardener and knowledgeable farmer.

It was an unusually hot summer as we waited for the giant Jubilee and Charleston Gray watermelons to ripen. I thought about the insurmountable task that lay ahead when it would be time to harvest them. It was a happy time for me, yet the heat was almost unbearable, as I faced the summer months since I was expecting our third child in September. Still the watermelons grew large and ripened just as Johnny was put on a 12 hour night shift. I put on very little weigh because I was busy canning and freezing vegetables from our garden and making strawberry jam from a patch that Mrs. Ryan had planted before she took a job as a baby sitter in Pensacola. When the crop of melons were ripe and ready to be picked, Johnny worked all night at Brookley Field, and then hired some young boys to help him pick and pile them under the Mimosa tree for the next three days.

After they were pulled, Johnny went to a shed in Foley where the tractor trailer trucks waited for farmers to engage them to haul their melons. The watermelons were selling for a nickel a pound the day they loaded over 29 tons on an 18 wheeler. Although he had been without sleep for sometime he reported back to work the next night. We were both exhausted after it was all over. I cooked dinner every day for the workers in my steaming hot kitchen and it seemed as soon as I got the dishes washed and the kitchen cleaned they all came back for supper. Those were the days before air conditioners, so with only one window fan, I still can feel the heat rising in that little kitchen.

I was worried about Johnny when it became his time to drive to work because he had not had much sleep. He carpooled with four or five local men. One day he got so sleepy he did not remember passing Malbis so one of the guys told him to pull over and let him drive. Several days later when Johnny was off work he went back for his check for the watermelons he sold. The buyers told him that the price had fallen to 1½ cents a pound not the 5 cents a pound he was promised when he loaded the truck. So goes, one of the hazards or disappointments of farming. For a city boy turned country, farming was now in his blood come what may. The country was in this city boy to stay. He enjoyed watching the crops grow and being outdoors so he was now an official farmer and as his wife I was destined to be *a farmer's wife* whether it was one of my biggest *dreams* or not.

11
A Typical Family Holiday

Daddy (center) with his children, Bernard, Marion, Jeanette and Ernest on Thanksgiving at his home in the woods.

Daddy did not stay in the big house by himself long after Blannie died. He could have stayed there as long as he lived, but it was too much house for him and he knew Blannie's heirs wanted control of it since it had once belonged to their parents. So he tore down an old barn, saved the lumber and built a smaller house in the woods on land he had inherited from Blannie. He was content to hunt, fish and plant vegetables to sell at his roadside stand. His late wife's relatives did not hesitate to take all the best quilts and heirlooms, expensive dishes and keepsakes. Daddy took the old iron bed-steds, appliances and other pieces of furniture they left and never looked back. When he went to hear the will read he learned that he only received one-sixth of the bank account. Unfortunately when he sold his house he put money in Blannie's account to improve the property her house stood on, but never had his name added to the account.

Daddy later married Mrs. Lillie Story who was a plain country woman who never needed much except her sweet snuff and plenty of flour to make biscuits. Her dipping never bothered Daddy because he also dipped. All of us called her "Miss Lillie." She and Daddy made good companions because they worked together planting and gathering vegetables which they sold from their stand down by the busy highway. They were both early-birds in the morning and Miss Lillie believed in cooking breakfast even if Daddy did not want any. He had worked in the slaughter house so long he never could eat breakfast but needed his coffee. If we did not get out of bed when she had breakfast ready she would rattle the pots and pans until we did, or go to the door and call to Daddy's birddog. She would throw her a biscuit and say, "Turn around Bessie and catch this biscuit. On her command Bessie learned to turn around three times and then leap up in the air for her treat.

Miss Lillie was a talker. She enjoyed telling stories of her past. I would listen intently as she told about the years she worked in a cotton mill near her home in Sylacauga. I laughed when she referred to her supervisor as "The Super." She enjoyed watching wrestling so much she would have to leave the kitchen when we were cooking supper on Saturday night so she could yell for her favorite wrestler. It all seemed so real to her and she really fussed at the wrestler's opponent if she thought he was hurting her favorite guy. We told her once that they were just pretending or faking it, but she would have none of that. It was real to her. She kept the house clean and their clothes washed and mended and then sat up at night piecing quilts after Daddy was asleep. It was Miss Lillie who encouraged Daddy to put up sheetrock in the little house in the woods and hang some bedroom doors for privacy. After they painted the sheetrock she hung plastic curtains in the bare windows and bought pretty oil cloths for the table. Her crocheted doilies on the furniture and chenille bedspreads added a woman's touch to the inside of the house. Johnny supplied a bathroom sink and toilet and helped Daddy construct a bathroom but they never got a shower or hot water heater. They made do without these conveniences.

As time passed, the women of the family spent more time planning the Thanksgiving menu because the family was growing. Sometimes it was hard to find a place for everyone to sleep on Thanksgiving Eve, but some of the children enjoyed staying with their Uncle Bernard and Aunt Ethel's children. The problem at Daddy's house was getting the dogs quieted down so we could get to sleep. We did not rest much anyway considering we were sleeping on an old lumpy mattress with one child in between us, but we did not complain.

It was always hard to sleep smelling that sweet aroma of Rachel's turkey baking in the oven. On Thanksgiving morning we sat around the big table chopping ingredients for dressing and giblet gravy as we caught up on all the happenings since we last saw each other. Ethel made wonderful pumpkin pies made from fresh pumpkin and Marion's wife, Jeanette cooked the vegetables and lots of desserts. Rachel hardly ever failed to bring a cake she had perfected. It was a yellow layer cake with caramel icing that was out of this world.

Now it was the big bucks the men charged through the woods in pursuit of because they became more plentiful than quail. I believed their deer drives were dangerous because one man would walk with the dogs on the drive as they drove the deer from their hiding places. Johnny gradually began to replace the bird dogs with deer dogs. He bought some beagle puppies to train to chase deer on their drives. Each man took a stand in a certain area and waited in hopes the dogs would run a deer by them. After the men and boys returned at noon telling stories of who shot a deer, who missed one and needed their shirt tail cut off and the one that got away, we finally sat down to a Thanksgiving feast. There was not enough room to seat the children at the table when they were small. Daddy's daily newspapers came in handy as we spread them on the linoleum so the children could eat their dinner. Our family was growing as our children started marrying and began families of their own. Every year there was a new spouse or baby to be introduced to the family. The younger children enjoyed playing in the clean raked yard since "Miss Lillie" never let any grass grow in her yard. Daddy always swept it clean. There would be little truck tracks and roads all over the place. One day the kids got into Daddy's hot bed where he had sweet potato plants growing with a fire under it to keep the plants from freezing. They got into trouble over that incident. Those were the days when our family enjoyed such a close relationship and we all looked forward to the Thanksgiving holidays with such anticipation. That holiday was the highlight of our year. The togetherness we shared with one another was so special. Those of us who remain hold fond memories of thirty-five years of happy gatherings either at the big house by the busy highway or the little house in the woods that we still *dream* about to this day.

12
Temporary Duty Yonder

~~~~~~~~~~~~~~~

A Call to Peru

Affter we had been married for four years Johnny signed up to travel from Brookley Air Force Base to other states where bases needed additional men to get aircraft repaired quickly. He referred to the assignment to other bases as T.D.Y. (Temporary Duty Yonder). We saw it as a way to save some money since he was paid extra per-diem for living expenses. We had never owned a new car, but we realized he would need a reliable vehicle in order to make the long trips. In 1956 we purchased a new yellow and white Pontiac Catalina. Of course, it did not have power steering, air conditioning, electric seats and windows, seatbelts, cruise control and all the other extra amenities we expect in a car today, but it was brand new, carried six people comfortably and had a large trunk; plus we thought it was the most superb looking car we had ever seen.

The first time I drove the Pontiac to Robertsdale for groceries I was apprehensive because Blackwater Bridge on Highway 90 was a narrow wooden bridge with wooden rails on the sides and I was afraid I was going to sideswipe a big truck. There had been a lot of dangerous wrecks on the bridge with cars plunging into the water and some fatalities and I was fearful I would meet a car on it. The Pontiac seemed so much wider than the Studebaker I was used to driving but I managed to avoid hitting anyone.

We still only had one child in the spring of 1956, so Barry and I were able to travel with Johnny on his first assignment. After Easter in April when the azaleas and wisteria were in full bloom we left a mild climate in Alabama. We arrived in Peru, Indiana two days later, only to wake up to a heavy snow the next morning. We rented a nice trailer in a trailer park full of friendly neighbors where Barry looked forward to watching a train with endless boxcars pass on the other side of the road every day. We were beginning to get to know the neighbors and were enjoying their company. We had been there only two weeks when the owners of the trailer returned home and needed it so we had to move. The only place Johnny could find to rent was a two-room apartment in the older town of Peru, Indiana. Since we had to move immediately, he rented it over the telephone sight unseen.

When we parked at the rental building I took one look at the old brick building and shivers went up my spine because it looked very spooky and unattended. I was astounded when we carried our luggage from the car, climbed the high steps to a door that opened into a dark hallway floor. The well worn rug that spanned the length of the hall appeared old and dirty as we checked door numbers looking for the apartment we would inhabit for the remainder of our trip. We opened the door and switched on the light only to see a number of roaches scurrying about on the floor. I wanted to run back to the car and not subject my child to such a dirty dingy apartment that evidently had not been cleaned in months. I set the luggage on the bed and laid out clean sheets and pillow cases while Johnny hurried to purchase some roach spray, disinfectant and cleaning supplies. He sprayed the entire room while we dozed in the car waiting for the odor to diminish.

I realized I would have plenty of time to clean, but I felt uneasy at night sharing the community bathroom with strangers living in the other apartments on each side of the long hallway. The next day I cleaned the kitchen area, refrigerator, and stove and washed all the dishes and cooking utensils before I would use them. After mopping and dusting I tackled the big bathroom that looked as if it had not been cleaned and disinfected in months. I calculated that all the renters must be men since they never cleaned it after using it.

Then there was nothing to do, but take the laundry down the street to the Laundromat and browse through the dime store or take Barry to the ice cream parlor every evening. My excitement about living in a small old town in Indiana was short lived. However, I was there to cook our meals so Johnny did not have to eat out. I still got an eerie feeling when I took my bath and bathed Barry during the day although I believed the other occupants of the building must all be away at work. He was still small so I took him with me to the bathroom and let him play on the clean floor while I bathed and shampooed my hair. I never let him out of my sight. I could not put off getting my bath until Johnny got home because I had to have supper ready and clean the kitchen then. The main thing was that the rent was low so we were saving money to pay on the car and purchase more land to farm later on. We did not have a television set at home so we did not miss that means of entertainment. I played games with Barry and read the books over and over that I had taken with me. I never met any of the renters, but heard them as they moved up and down the halls of that strange old apartment house, early in the mornings. It was a happy day for me when the time came for us to return to our little country home in Elsanor, Alabama. I wondered what the next town would hold and if there would be more unpleasant circumstances. Peru, Indiana, had not proved to be my ideal rustic *dream* town.

13
Off to Ohio

When Johnny was traveling from Brookley AFB to work on aircraft in other states he would be away for several months so I considered it a vacation for me and Barry to go along. During March of 1957 we packed up and left in the Pontiac for Columbus, Ohio. We found Columbus to be a much larger town than Peru, Indiana. It had several downtown movie theatres and nice stores for shopping. We were not interested in restaurants because we only ate out when traveling. Another fellow aircraft mechanic made the trip with us. He needed a ride and helped buy the gasoline, so I relinquished the front seat of the car and my job as navigator. Barry and I were comfortable in the back seat, but at times felt nauseous during the long trip. I had a reason that riding in the back seat around the mountains and curves was causing motion sickness. Barry usually rode up front with us and was fine so it did not occur to me that he was also having motion sickness. I later decided if we rode in the back seat again, I would get some Dramamine to take along. We drank a lot of Seven-Up and ate very little.

Even though it was a little battered, Barry wore his little black cowboy hat that Santa brought him the previous Christmas. When we stopped at a restaurant I tried to get him to part with the cowboy hat until we returned to the car, but he would not leave it. I thought people would wonder why we could not afford to buy him a better looking hat but I now know that it was one of his prized possessions and it did not matter what the people we saw in that restaurant thought because we would never see them again.

As soon as we arrived in Columbus we bought a newspaper and began looking for an apartment. After a weary day's search with no luck, we were down to the last advertisement so we hurriedly made the call. An elderly lady answered the phone and informed us she had not rented her apartment. She gave John her address and directions to her home because she wanted to interview us. She invited us into her living room and we found her to be very cordial and friendly. I informed her I would keep the apartment immaculate and our rent payment would be on time every month. We breathed a prayer that the landlady rented us the apartment because we were so tired and desperately needed a place to get settled in before John checked in at Lockbourne AFB (now Rickenbacker AFB) the next day.

After we answered the landlady's questions she was satisfied that we were respectable people and agreed to let us have the apartment. We gladly paid a month's rent and signed the lease. This time we climbed the stairs to a cozy apartment with a clean kitchen and dining area and a large room where we slept and relaxed. Barry had plenty of space to play with his toys. I read lots of children's books to him and told him stories when it was naptime. Barry had a new imaginary friend that he referred to as Michael who accompanied him on fishing trips and other day time excursions. I marveled at some of the unique places they traveled and things a two-year-old could make up. We took an alarm radio that we often turned on in order to get the news and weather. My pastimes were crocheting and reading after my work was done. However, I never learned to master baby booties and caps as I did the delicate pineapple and wheat doilies. I did my laundry in an adjoining attic and hung the clothes on lines in there. It took two or three days for them to dry. One day a pigeon found its way in the attic and I had to shoo him out before he ruined my clean laundry.

We awakened to an unexpected blanket of snow one morning. We looked out the window to the most beautiful winter wonderland snow scene. Everything was so white that it compared to a picture on a calendar; but I also knew it meant confinement for me and Barry and trouble for Johnny driving to work without snow chains. But we coped as it snowed several days. John bought the snow chains and I enjoyed the one-on-one time with my son. As time went by I began to miss my Alabama friends, but at least they corresponded with me. When I went down stairs to check the mail on the porch I met the lady who lived on the first floor. She had a little boy, so we struck up a conversation that turned into a friendship. After the snow melted and the temperature rose, my new friend put her baby in the stroller and we took walks to the park to let the children play. We were happy to be out in the fresh air after several days of cabin fever.

After John got in from work or when he had a day off we did the usual grocery shopping so I could cook all our meals and make his lunch every day. I woke up early and prepared a hot breakfast before he went to the base for a long day's work. One of the things I missed was not being able to buy grits to cook for breakfast, but found rice would substitute just as well. The clerks in the grocery stores did not seem to know what grits were. Since the weather was so cold we sometimes caught a movie at a downtown theatre and shopped a little, but we held to our goal of saving money so we bought nothing extravagant and spent little on entertainment.

It was June when we left Ohio one afternoon to return to our Alabama home. Johnny and his friend wanted to get home as soon as possible so we drove straight through the night. It proved to be a hard trip for me because I was so stiff when we stopped. My back and hips hurt from sitting so long until I could hardly walk when we did stop for gasoline. Although I was just as anxious as Johnny to get home I asked him to get a motel room for a few hours rest but he did not want to spend money for a motel bill when we could keep traveling throughout the night.

But the worse was yet to come. We arrived home just before day break to an overgrown yard and a house full of mildew. I was shocked when I saw how high the grass in the yard was and terrified there were snakes everywhere. Friends later told us it had rained almost every day while we were away. As tired as I was, sleep would not come because all I could think of was snakes. We had our work cut out for us and vowed never to go off again without hiring the grass cut and the house aired out. So ended another enjoyable TDY trip, that we considered a *dream* vacation.

14
A Second Gift from Heaven

Pictured is baby Doyle Gene
Ryan at 2 months of age.

His big brother Barry
gets a hug.

We decided to cancel our travels until after our baby was born. Doyle came into the world on July 2, 1957. I had been canning soup the day before I went to the hospital in Mobile, so I kept telling Johnny to get me some more corn for my soup when I was sedated. Dr. R. E. Abell was a wonderfully skilled gynecologist so I felt so much better after the baby's birth. I was not over sedated during his birth because I remember the terrific pains I felt and remembered the nurses giving me instructions before they gave me more anesthesia. The doctor knew that I would be better off to suffer during the birthing than later on as I had done before. Johnny insisted on naming the baby Doyle Gene, but he did not tell me why he liked the name until years later. It was because his sister, Elsie, had dated a prize fighter named Doyle Gene before she met her husband and he liked the fighter. My neighbor said Doyle was too cute to be a boy, but he was a good baby and slept all night after he came home from the hospital. We would wait until Doyle was old enough to travel before we made any more TDY trips. I wondered where the yellow and white Pontiac would take us when we set out again to temporary duty yonder. I was content at the time to stay home and rock the baby while Barry played with his little cowboys, Indians and horses. But I still dreamed of traveling to other states and to be able to save a little more money to help pay for land and to construct a new home someday.

15
Oklahoma! Here We Come

Oil Wells in front of Capital

Train at Frontier City

O K Saloon at Frontier
City Park

Barry at age four in cowboy suit his dad bought

Doyle age 4 wearing same suit

Twila, age four, wearing her boots, cowgirl outfit and holster and pistol

Since I had been a country girl the entire 23 years of my life, I often thought it would be interesting to live in the suburbs of a city. So, when Johnny was sent on a temporary duty assignment to Tinker AFB in Midwest City, Oklahoma he rented us a modest house in a typical family subdivision and then returned to Alabama for me and the kids. I felt like I was living the American dream. The house and kitchen was completely furnished so all we took was our bed linens and towels. There was a modern washing machine in the utility room, whereas I had an older ringer type washer at home. I did not miss not having a clothes dryer because I did not have one at home and I liked hanging the laundry out in the sun anyway. The only means of cooling our little house in Elsanor was a big window fan, but this house had a large unit in the living room window that was referred to as a water cooler. It automatically blew cold air into the living room and cooled the entire house. That air cooler made our nighttime slumber comfortable.

We found a church we enjoyed attending and the welcome committee ladies visited the next day. It was nice having the milkman bring the milk to my door every morning and the ice cream man come down the street playing his music so my boys could enjoy an afternoon snack. The kids had so much fun looking through the garage of the rental house where so many toys and other things were stored.

The proprietor told us to use what we wanted, so the boys especially enjoyed the little swimming pool we set up in the back yard. One warm day the boys were playing in the wading pool with the next door neighbor's son who was older than they were. The back yard was fenced-in so I thought there was no way they could get out but I was proved wrong. I was out there hanging clothes as I watched them play but had to step inside the house for a minute to check on something I was cooking. Suddenly, I heard a loud horn blowing in the street out front. Johnny and I both hurried out the front door to see our one year old son, Doyle, standing dripping wet in his diaper in the middle of the street. I did not have a bathing suit for Doyle so he played in the water in his Birdseye diaper. The little boy next door had climbed the gate, unlocked it from the top, went home and left the gate open. Doyle decided he would take a tour of the neighborhood. I thanked God the lady was able to stop and Doyle was not hit. We secured the gate better at the top from then on.

Johnny worked long hours so I had time to get acquainted with the neighbors living on each side of us. I made friends with the single mother who lived on the right of our house and although she did not have time for coffee and cake in the mornings, I would go over and visit her and clean her kitchen while my boys played with her kids. In order to make a living and be a stay-at-home mom she took in ironing. She stood on her feet ironing from early morning until late at night. I felt sorry for her because she never had time to go anywhere or play with her kids. I could not imagine ironing starched clothes all day long even though I ironed our starched clothes one day during the week. My other next door neighbor worked, but we visited during the afternoons and she gave us a lot of nectarines from her tree.

One beautiful summer Sunday afternoon we all loaded up in the '56 Pontiac and drove a few miles from Midwest City to check out a local attraction because we thought the kids would enjoy seeing a little western town. Our son, Barry, was especially interested in anything western since he enjoyed playing cowboys and Indians. When we arrived at Frontier City we found a small western village that put on shows and entertainment for the tourists. One of their western shows was about to begin, so we hurriedly bought tickets and found seats on the bleachers. It was a regular knock-down, drag-out battle among the gunfighters. I almost screamed out when Wyatt Earp shot Doc Holiday on top of the OK Saloon and he fell to the ground during one of the scenes. At the end of the show all of the bad gunslingers were lying on the ground.

We toured a little shop where Johnny bought Barry a cowboy suit with brown pants and a gold shirt with fringe that made him one happy four year old kid. I thought $8.00 was too much to splurge for a cowboy suit, when he was outgrowing his other clothes, but I could not foresee then that all three of my children would enjoy wearing this outfit for years to come. It never wore out so that was money well spent and also brought a lot of pleasure to our kids. I always regretted complaining because I would have denied all of my children many happy hours of innocent play.

It was 1958 when we visited Frontier City. At that time it was a small village with a miniature train that carried sightseers around on a track, but today it is Oklahoma's largest theme park located on 40 acres with 50 rides and attractions including 4 roller coasters and 2 water rides. But the Wild West gunfighter's stunt show is still a favorite side show.

The landlord would stop by the house to check on things and service the water cooler. He took note that I had gotten down on my hands and knees and waxed the hardwood floors because they were scratched. I wanted them to shine when our friend, Jerry Stastka from Elsanor, came for supper one Sunday night. Jerry, who also worked at Brookley AFB, was sent to Oklahoma to attend an aircraft school concerning testing jet engines while we were there. We looked forward to seeing him and catching up on all the news from our community and church. I remembered he liked homemade ice cream, so after supper we tried out Johnny's electric freezer he bought at the big auction. It worked like a charm.

After three or four months the Alabama men had finished their job at Tinker Field and it was time for us to head home. Johnny's mother missed her other grandchildren and we needed to get home to see about our property and resume our lives. So, the city mouse had to return to the home where she would once again take up her role as a wife and mother as the country mouse. I could not believe my eyes when I witnessed Johnny packing every bit of the stuff he bought at the auction along with our clothes and other belongings in the trunk of the car. We even brought a canary home from Oklahoma along with a large rug, swivel chairs for the boys, and other useful items. Now it's funny when I think about how I wanted to live in the suburbs of a big city. As I grew older I was perfectly content to live in the country on a farm with a beautiful view of the flowers, birds and butterflies in my back yard. The trees lining the swamp and the glorious sunsets with such beautiful colors that cannot be described, lifts me up. I can see the cows as they graze from my den window and the cardinals and hummingbirds feed at the feeders and I feel so humbled. My children bought me two birdbaths for the birds to splash in. We placed them near the red geraniums planted in old black iron wash pots.

I watch the pigeons swoop and circle as they take their afternoon flight when Johnny turns them out for their exercise. I stand in amazement because of the homing instinct they have shown as they flew long races. Of course, there have been long days of hard work when I was younger when I wished I could change places with the ladies in towns who visited each other in the mornings to drink coffee and play cards at luncheons, but not anymore. I just go outside and look at my beautiful crepe myrtles blooming along the roadside and the spacious yard full of green grass and a variety of flowers blooming and I "Thank God, I'm a Country Girl." I no longer want to live in a crowded subdivision where all the homes are close together and they all look the same because I am happy here on this farm. I am content and my dreams are complete and fulfilled.

16
Fun in Florida

Jeanette and Johnny playing with boys in water at Panama City, FL.

The cabin we stayed in is in the background close to the beach.

Barry playing in yard at Panama City

Johnny relaxes after work with his boys

The summer of 1960 Johnny got his TDY orders to report to Tyndall AFB in Panama City, Florida, to work on drones. I knew at once I wanted to go on this trip with him because it may very well be the last one I could take. Our oldest son, Barry, would be six years old in July and I would need to stay home and keep him in school instead of traipsing all over the country. Most of the trips I had accompanied Johnny on had been interesting and enjoyable. We had been blessed to find decent places to live except for the dirty, insect-infested apartment in Indiana. I enjoyed Oklahoma so much and knew if we could find a beach cottage in Panama City with reasonable rent that would make for a terrific fun summer for all of us even if Johnny had to work during the day.

After going down to report for work the first week and look for a place for us to stay, he hit the jackpot. He found a small cottage just a few feet from the water on a long beach with gleaming white sand. The water was calm and suitable for swimming, floating on our rafts and boating and the beach was smooth and wonderful for the kids to play on and for long walks. The boys were so excited. Barry had graduated from being a make-believe cowboy and was now a full fledged U. S. Army man. Every day he would pull the old Air Force backpack over his shoulders that his dad had given him, hook his canteen on his belt, put on an old safari hat that substituted for his army helmet, gather up his play rifles and binoculars he received for Christmas and head for the outdoors with his three-year old brother, Doyle, dressed in his army fatigue shirt and pants, trailing behind.

The boys usually played in the corner of our front yard under a Mimosa tree that their grandmother Ryan planted. The tree bloomed radiant pink flowers in June and provided shade and a place for the kids to climb. However, it soon became headquarters for an army fort. I did not worry about them climbing the tree and falling because it was not very tall. Not much traffic came down the lane because it was a dead end lane so if anyone came they were coming to see us and watched for the children. If cousins or friends came to visit they were immediately introduced to Fort Ryan. Things went along fine until one day they found the shovel and decided to dig a big foxhole under the tree. The boys and their cousins had a grand old time playing army and protecting their fort with their play rifles until Johnny came driving down the lane from work. He ordered them to fill up that hole and smooth the dirt down.

From then on they played with the many Army soldiers, tanks

and airplanes in the soft dirt of the garage. They graded the roads with their Tonka road graders and hauled the dirt in their Tonka dump trucks until it was time for their Daddy to come home and put the Pontiac in the garage. Sure, they got dirty, had sand in their hair and sandworms in their feet, but the dirt washed off and we got rid of the cat while the doctor froze the sand worms. Those were the days of carefree play and happy days of imaginative games without much T.V. I am glad I did not restrict them from getting dirty.

Our relatives from North Alabama would stop by to see us on their way to Panama City for vacations, and I would think how nice it would be to vacation there. We never could afford it, so this trip was like another dream come true. A paid summer vacation in Panama City right on the water was going to be fun. The boys were a little older this time and were excited to be able to live in the four room bungalow on the beach. Although Johnny had to work long hours the boys and I hit the beach every morning, came in to eat a sandwich and rest at noon and went back to the water later that afternoon. We enjoyed floating on the big floaters and since Johnny had taken a small boat with us; he took us for boat rides if he came home early. Another family from Brookley AFB rented a cabin next door so the boys had a lot of fun playing with their little boy while I sat in the sandy shady backyard and visited with his mom while watching the squirrels play in the trees. The only place we went was grocery shopping and to church on Sunday nights because Johnny had to work some Sundays. Many wonderful fun-filled days called to us just outside our door.

We settled in the cabin and before we knew it, it was July and Barry's and Doyle's birthdays were approaching. We invited Elsie and Biddle and their five kids in Pensacola to come help us celebrate the fourth of July, and enjoy a day of picnicking and swimming. Johnny bought the biggest 50 pound watermelon we had ever seen and we enjoyed eating it after lunch. They got there early and stayed late that Sunday.

I met many friendly people on both sides of the street and took leisurely walks on the beach with the boys as we looked for shells. I hurriedly did the housework and cooking each day so we could spend more time on the beach and in the water. I am sure if we took a vacation to Panama City now it would really be expensive and not as much fun as it was when we were all young. The summer we spent there in 1960 was cheap and we had a fantastic time. When it was time to come home we sported dark tans and counted our blessing that we had a wonderful free summer vacation on the beach and even saved money. Johnny never complained about the long hours and hard work because he seemed to be more content when he was working. Of all the TDY trips we made this one was the best dream vacation of all.

17
Trips to Other Bases

~~~~~~~~~

Johnny made several other short trips to different bases on short notice. Once we went to Birmingham and we were able to stay with his Aunt Maggie Nichols who was his mother's sister. She lived on the outskirts of the city and I will never forget that we walked through her front door on level ground, then through her living room and kitchen and out on her back porch only to look down and see a steep drop-off. Her house was truly built on the side of a mountain. I watched Barry closely because I was afraid that he would fall off the porch and roll down that steep hill. It was nice visiting Johnny's other relatives while we were there.

Once he was called to work at Hulbert Field at Ft. Walton Beach, Florida so he traveled back and forth to work. At the time Johnny was installing plywood and new tile on our floors because the old linoleum was so cracked and worn out. After driving home on weekends he would lay tile until late at night. He would lay as much tile as he could and rise early Monday morning and drive back to Ft. Walton. I was so happy to have the new tile on the floors even if it was not expensive. I could then mop and wax the floors and the rooms looked so much better. I began to paint all of the walls and put up new curtains. Our little improvement effort made a big difference. We hired a man to put the gray siding on the outside of the house and we painted the windows.

Yes, the old yellow and white Pontiac served us well and carried us many miles to different states on government assignments and kept us safe and well so Johnny could do the job he was trained for and help the government. By traveling to these jobs we were able to save enough money to purchase land that would be of value to farm in the future and help us construct our home. Johnny stopped traveling for the government shortly after Barry started school. Over the years we would purchase many other models of cars such as the light blue luxury Ford LTD, the red sporty Ford Maverick that I drove to work for nine years, the two Mercury Marquis's that drove like a dream. We also enjoyed owning several older models of Cadillac's and our latest, Lincoln Town car; plus many new farm trucks, but our memories of the good times spent in different states where our dependable 1956 Pontiac took us remains in our hearts. Our family had seen the towns of Peru, Indiana and Columbus, Ohio, blanketed in snow, visited oil wells in front of Oklahoma's capital city, toured a western theme park and village and topped it off playing in the blue/green crystal waters of Panama City, Florida. Plus we were able to live comfortably and save money. What more could we ask for? We were happy and free in the good old USA and never wanted to go overseas. We traveled through several states and lived in states that we never *dreamed* we would see, much less live in.

18
Prayers Answered: "It's a girl"

 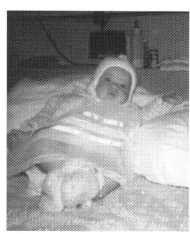

Our third child was a precious little girl

Doyle and Barry helped take care
of their sister

It was a long hot summer and it seemed I stayed in that hot kitchen cooking for Johnny's workers so much; I thought I would never be cool again. Even the nights were scorching and the window fan did not help much since we had to open the window where the boys slept so they could feel a little breeze. Day after day the temperatures soared and the air remained hot. I slept at the foot of the bed to try to get more air. The indigestion I was having day and night was not helping matters. I was expecting our third child and prayed every day that it would be a girl but we had no way of knowing because in 1962 I had never heard of sonograms.

I had not gained much weight because I did not have much of an appetite. Little did I know then that it was the iron tablets that the doctor prescribed that was making me sick with indigestion. However, the baby and I both needed the iron supplement because I always lost a jaw tooth after each baby was born. I clearly remember how hard it was to stoop over to pick the vegetables from the garden and the strawberries from a little patch that Granny Ryan had planted. About the time they were ready she found a job in Pensacola baby sitting a little boy, so she was not there to pick them. However, the jam and jelly I made from them was worth the discomfort.

The date was September 19, 1962. I was twenty-nine years old and most miserable yet very excited as we awaited the birth of our third child. We had turned the small nursery that baby Doyle occupied into a closet and sewing room when Johnny purchased my new portable Singer sewing machine. Johnny then built a small room for a nursery that joined our bedroom on the other side for our newly expected bundle of joy. So when the time approached for the arrival of our new addition Johnny was busy putting a fresh coat of paint on the walls and the old crib that we had used for the boys. I could hardly wait to fix up the nursery and get it organized. He had worked all day at his job and began painting as soon as supper was over therefore he was pretty tired when we finally lay down for the night. It took me awhile to drift off to sleep with the room filled with strong paint odor. Around midnight I was awakened with a hard labor pain so I had to wake Johnny as bad as I hated to. I told him that we had better go on across the causeway to the Mobile Infirmary since we lived 50 miles from the hospital.

When I got to the hospital the nurse weighed me in at 132 pounds and questioned me if I was sure it was my due date. I told her I was sure. So they gave me a shot in order to give Dr. Abel a little more sleep. I was out from then on and I knew nothing until the nurse woke me and told me that I had a little girl. On a cool September morning around 6:00 am of 1962 our little baby girl was born. The nurse kept telling me to wake up and see my new baby girl. I thought I was dreaming because I had been praying so long for a little girl to dress up and make pretty ribbons for her hair. I remember groggily asking the nurse was she sure the baby was a girl. I had slept through the entire delivery and had suffered no pain. Dr. Abel came into my room and told me and the lady in the other bed that we had really kept him busy. Both our babies were coming at the same time and he was running from place to place. We named our daughter, Twila, after one of Johnny's Air Force buddy's wife who lived in California. I immediately started making cute little dresses and blankets for her, but would have to wait awhile to make ribbons until her hair grew some because she did not have any hair. This little bundle of joy made our family complete. Doyle was a big help because he had not yet started school. He played with her and talked to her as she lay in the crib while I hung out the clothes. At five years old I could trust him to let me know if I needed to hurry into the house.

Barry was in the second grade when Twila was born. When he went to school his teacher questioned him as to what we had named his new little sister. He had never heard of the name "Twila" so he could not remember. When he came home that evening he asked me to write it on a piece of paper so he could give it to Mrs. Scruggs. Life was getting busier than ever but I did not mind since we had been blessed with three healthy children. Johnny and I had been married 11 years and needed more space because the walls were bulging out, but I knew when God was ready and the time was right He would provide us with a new house with plenty of closets and bedrooms for these little gifts from above. So until that day, I would hold the secret *dreams* in my heart never doubting that Johnny would keep the promise he made me before we married that someday he would build me a new house.

The good news was that while I was in the hospital Johnny found his mother a used trailer and parked it in the back yard so she could set up housekeeping and we could keep an eye on her and help with her needs. I do not know who was more relieved, Mrs. Ryan or me. She had lived with us for 11 difficult years. Now our little house and her small trailer were our separate homes to fix up as we pleased. The only problem was that Granny was afraid to stay by herself at night and wanted Doyle to stay with her. When she received her little

Railroad Retirement check she bought moon pies and different kinds of cereal that he liked so he would be tempted to go over for his night time snack. When he came home for breakfast he smelled like smoke. I worried that her cigarette smoking was unhealthy for him.

Both of our dreams of having our own domain where we would not get into discussions about what to cook for supper or how to arrange the furniture had come true. Actually, Granny Ryan enjoyed working outdoors and stayed busy planting flowers, shrubs and trees around the house while I had rather stay inside and clean and cook so that was a good arrangement. I did not have a green thumb, but everything she planted or tried to root survived and flourished. That was one of her talents and a good thing, but I often wondered why she could love flowers so much and not even like her daughter-in-law. If only we could have had a relationship such as the one described in the Bible between Naomi and her daughter-in-law Ruth. Maybe it was my fault as much as hers. There would never be a close relationship between me and Johnny's mother which was so sad because life would have been much more pleasurable if only we could have loved each other instead of tolerated the years we spent together. But no matter how hard I tried I was never able to please her.

19
Family Times Together

Johnny and the boys show their baby sister their new Tonka trucks and let her sit on one. Sage grass field is in the background.

1962, was the Year of crew cuts, bow ties, white shirts, ladies Easter hats, beads and homemade dresses.

Barry with Easter basket

Doyle waiting to hunt eggs

Twila in her Easter dress

Left: Easter at the Little House
Pictured are Granny Ryan, Barry,
Sylvia, Patsy, Bill and Libby
Howell, Jeanette and Ethel Dyess

Right: A Picnic down by the
ponds under the oaks on Easter
Sunday meant good food and
Easter egg hunts while others
relaxed and enjoyed the day.

E aster Sunday was one of my favorite holidays and I started making plans early to invite relatives to spend the day at our house. The fact that it was small did not bother me because I knew that Elsie and Biddle and their family would enjoy coming to the country for dinner even if some of us had to eat in the yard. God smiled on us at Easter because I cannot remember it ever raining when Johnny's family joined us on Easter Sunday. We met at our house after attending church to commemorate the day our Savior arose from the dead. We usually made some pictures before we took off our Easter outfits and hats. Granny Ryan and I began cooking on Saturday in order to have plenty of food to add to the dinner the other families brought. On Saturday afternoon I boiled the eggs and called the children in to decorate them. This was always a special time of stopping my busy schedule to spend time with the kids. It was a lesson in letting them be creative and decorate their own special eggs while I explained to them why we celebrated Easter. Ruth and Otto and their family usually joined us for Easter, and on occasion, my brother, Bernard and his family came when they lived in Seminole. I thoroughly enjoyed company. My motto was, "The more the merrier." We had a large yard and lots of space for hiding and hunting eggs.

After we moved to the new house Johnny built ponds in order to furnish water for the cattle. For several years we had Easter picnics down there under the big oaks that would just be budding out. We began to invite other relatives from both families and everyone brought their favorite dishes to compliment the turkey and ham I cooked. I especially remember the times my Aunt Ora Mae and Uncle Jessie from Mobile joined us and the Peckhams who were my daughter-in-law, Charlene's family. As the grandchildren came along we picked out one special spot under the oak trees to hide the eggs. One of Patti and Ricky Peckham's little boys was hunting for eggs and tripped over a dried cow patty spilling his eggs. Not knowing what to do he just lay there on the ground surrounded by pretty colored eggs. Everyone grabbed their cameras. He was so small he could not remember the incident the next year but someone always told the story. He took it all in stride as he was reminded the next year to watch where he stepped. We usually tried to make a trip to get Daddy to visit during Easter. As we aged it got harder for Johnny to scrape and clean under the trees and to transport tables and food to our favorite picnic spot so we discontinued meeting there and met at our home. When our grandchildren were older we bought them a large swing set and slide and surprised them with it one Easter Sunday. They enjoyed playing on it for many years. After we moved, it did rain one year so the children hunted eggs hidden in the hay in Johnny's newest barn. Today our children take turns hosting all the other holidays, but Christmas is still celebrated at the farm. I get dreamy when I think about the happy Easters we spent hunting eggs with grandchildren when they were small.

20
The Hunt for the Perfect Cedar Tree

Barry checking out gifts
from Santa

Jeanette and boys by Christmas
tree in 1957

Our little family of four

Twila and Doyle check out toys
on Christmas

On Sunday afternoons about two weeks before Christmas our family hurried home from church for a quick lunch I had prepared ahead of time. I knew the kids would be anxious to pile into the old pickup truck and head for the woods and riverbanks to look for a Christmas tree. After lunch I bundled them up to face the chilly weather. It would not be an easy task finding a nice straight cedar tree. Sometimes Johnny discovered a larger tree that he could cut the top out of that we could decorate with the few ornaments and tinsel we had. Money was scarce in the 1960's and most of our friends did not buy expensive well developed trees either. We needed all the money we could scrape up for gifts for the kids. Our children had never experienced receiving lavish gifts because they were content with small things such as a gun and holster set, a cowboy hat and boots for the boys and a doll and buggy for Twila until she began to want cowboy stuff and play horses, too.

The entire family was so excited the day Mr. Virgil Bodle brought a new Motorola black and white television set to our house. I especially enjoyed watching the Christmas specials with Bob Hope and other celebrity comedians such as Red Skelton, Jack Benny, Gracie and George Burns and others. The kids would sit as long as I would let them and watch "Captain Kangaroo, or their favorite cartoon show. Barry and Doyle especially enjoyed seeing "The Lone Ranger" and other cowboy shows. Johnny had very little time to watch T.V. but one Sunday night when he was working overtime on the night shift I have to confess that the boys and I skipped church. We did however have a good reason to stay home and watch "The Wizard of Oz." The county was preparing to pave our road that winter and I was apprehensive that I might get the truck stuck or slip in the ditch. I decided that the good Lord would forgive me for not taking the boys out in the pouring rain on such a dark night. The three of us sat glued to the television set until the show was over.

Those were the days of good clean television so I never had to check to see what they were watching. I cannot remember anything that was not appropriate for the kids to watch since they were not interested in the soaps or thriller shows. I will always remember the days of wonderful comedians, movies and day time game shows that were so much fun. I hurried to get through with supper and dishes so I could join them in the living room for a delightful night of "I Love Lucy" or "The Honeymooners." I wish we could return to those days of clean television shows without cursing or obscene situations that children do not need to hear or see. It is no wonder that some of the youth of today get into trouble. We can never return to those days when life was more innocent and carefree. We can only remember those days from the past in our *dreams*.

21
The Intruder and the Guest

~~~~~~~~~~~~~~~~~~~~~~~~~

On another cold Sunday the family was dressed for church when we heard the same rumbling in the attic that had kept us up most of Saturday night. Johnny thought since it made so much noise it must be a squirrel rolling around some pecans from our only pecan tree. The children and I ran out the door and hopped into the car when Johnny picked up his rifle. When he lifted the outside vent to try to see what was in the attic it was dark but he did catch a glimpse of what he thought was the squirrel so he fired. Immediately the strong odor of a skunk filled the house and the yard. Johnny avoided a direct hit of the skunk's fumes so he too ran to the car. We went on to church hoping and praying that we carried no skunk perfume with us on our clothes. After services we returned to a house that had such strong skunk scent that I could not cook lunch. If I did cook I knew we could not eat what I prepared.

Since all the eating places in town were closed on Sundays we pondered how we would feed the kids. Then we happened to remember that a small hamburger stand had opened on Highway 90 in our community. We never splurged on eating out, but this was an emergency. After opening all the windows in the house we drove to the stand where Johnny bought the burgers that we ate in the car. Later that afternoon we visited friends and relatives. It made no difference how much we dreaded going home to that smelly house we knew we had to return to spend the night there and somehow fumigate it.

Early Monday morning I began washing clothes, bed sheets, towels and everything affected by the stench. I mopped the floors with Lysol and sprayed an entire can of Lysol throughout the house but the skunk smell remained. On Monday evening while I was still busy scrubbing someone knocked on the door. When I went to the door I stood there in shock as I stared at Eddie Engler who had been one of Johnny's buddies in the Air Force in California. I thought to myself, "This cannot be happening." Eddie and his wife, Twila, had always been welcome in our home but I was so embarrassed that he had stopped by at such an inopportune time. With the house still reeking of skunk aroma I wondered, "What in the world will I do?" I quickly explained the situation to Eddie and told him he was welcome to come in and that Johnny would soon be home but if he chose not to enter our smelly house I would understand. He just laughed and came on in the door. Everything worked out in the end. The bad smell diminished some by late evening. I cooked supper and we were able to eat and Johnny and Eddie spent an enjoyable evening reminiscing about their stint in the Air Force. That night I *dreamed* even more of a new home free from varmints and rodents.

22
The Christmas Eve Accident

The boys were happy to finally get their bikes.

They took a ride on Barry's bike.

When the boys were older Johnny decided it was time for Barry to have a bicycle and Doyle a tricycle. So we bought them and hid them in the carport. He planned to assemble them on Christmas Eve night after the kids had gone to bed and were sound asleep. However, when Christmas Eve came he had to report to work because the base needed to get a certain airplane repaired and back in the air. I knew it would be a tight schedule because with the children to care for I was late with my Christmas baking and mixing the dressing to go with the baked hen I would prepare Christmas morning.

Just as I was making my favorite Seven Minute Frosting for a chocolate layer cake, my neighbor knocked on the door. Beatrice Bain was the only neighbor on our road who was fortunate enough to have a telephone, so I knew immediately that she was the bearer of some kind of unpleasant news. She said she had a call from the Base hospital that Johnny had injured his elbow and they were admitting him to the hospital. I panicked as to what I would do. Johnny's sisters and brothers-in-law lived in Pensacola so I wondered how I would get to the hospital to see him. I was hesitant to ask local friends to drive me as I knew they would be with their families celebrating Christmas Eve. I decided to go to Beatrice's house and call Ruth, to ask her and Otto to take me to Mobile to see Johnny. They came over immediately to take me to check on Johnny. Mrs. Ryan kept all of the grandchildren at my house.

When we arrived at the base hospital we found Johnny with a cast on his elbow and him raring to go home. He had seriously injured his elbow while working on an F-100 Thunderbird Fighter Jet. A torque wrench came apart and knocked his elbow out of place. The force of the heavy wrench chipped the bone as well. The doctor told Johnny he was admitting him and that he would need to stay overnight and maybe longer. Johnny declared to them that it was Christmas Eve and he had toys to assemble for his two boys and he was going home. The doctor finally compromised by promising him if he would stay overnight that he would think about dismissing him the next day so he could have Christmas dinner with his family.

I asked Ruth and Otto if they would come have Christmas dinner with us so we would not be alone in case Johnny did not make it home. I would put some gifts under the tree for the boys and hold the others until Johnny got home. They boys only received a few gifts since we purchased the new black and white television set, a new living room suit and a set of bunk beds for the boys. Just as Johnny's mother and I were putting dinner on the table on Christmas Day we heard a car drive up. We hurried to the door and saw a big black automobile with the Air Force insigne on the side. Johnny with his arm in a sling and a top Air Force officer were exiting the car. Johnny had talked the doctor into dismissing him and making arrangements for him to have someone drive him home so he could be with his family for the holiday. He was supposed to rest but Otto and his boys helped him assemble Barry's bicycle with training wheels and Doyle's tricycle. He played with the boys that afternoon and promised them as soon as it was dark he would shoot off some firecrackers and light up some sparklers. Instead of having a simple Christmas that year we had to deal with a work related accident and an injured husband, father and son. Johnny's elbow would later require two surgeries but he would face that in the future; so on this cold winter holiday his only *dream* was of coming home to spend Christmas Day with his family.

23
Stories of Our Lives

Barry plays with Speck in back yard

Doyle wore a leg brace for 14 months

Barry with his collection of model airplanes

Barry and Doyle with fish they caught

The children were growing so fast. The boys enjoyed playing with their big Tonka dump truck, road grader and other road equipment in the sand in the garage. When they finished playing with the toys Barry washed them off with the hose, dried them and put them under the twin bunk beds he and Doyle shared. Barry started school in 1960 and Doyle missed not having anyone to play with. Then two years later when his little sister was born he was a big help to me. When I needed to hang clothes I would put Twila in the playpen and Doyle entertained her until I was through.

When Barry was six or seven he had the experience of seeing Granny Ryan deal with a situation that he thought hilarious at the time. Since Johnny needed worms for fishing he made a worm bed behind the wash house that was located near the coups where he raised his quail, pheasants and turkeys. One morning as he was leaving for work he noticed that something had dug in his worm bed and eaten a lot of his worms. He saw the troublesome varmint that morning but had no time to deal with it. He had seen these despicable looking things while stationed in Texas but that was the first one he had ever seen in our neck of the woods. He told me to warn his mother and the boys not to mess with this worm eater if they saw him. He would take care of it when he got home. Well, that news got his mother's curiosity up so she decided to look into the matter. Barry was out in the yard when she spotted the awful looking critter that she had never seen before. She hastily grabbed a metal Stanley mop handle and began beating the hard shell of the invader. Since Granny had a bad knee that was twisting because of arthritis she usually carried a cane and moved slowly but Barry observed from a distance that his Granny fought as if her life depended on her conquering this unnamed animal. She was at war. Sometimes she would think she got the best of it but then it would recover and run from her. By this time Barry was holding his sides from laughing so hard. Finally Granny won the battle in the end but she was worn to a frazzle with sweat pouring from her body. She told Barry he had better not say a word about her confrontation with whatever the thing was called. That dead armadillo would not dig in our yard again, but that was just the beginning of the zillions of armadillos that would pester us from that day forward.

I always had their birthday party on the same day because Barry was born on July 5th and Doyle on July 2nd. Usually I picked a convenient day between these dates for their party. The year Doyle turned six and Barry nine, I invited several children from church around the boy's ages. The mothers brought their kids and stayed for the combined birthday party. After we finished playing a couple of games I served the kids birthday cake and Kool-aid. Then the kids played on the swing set and slide and ran around in the yard. Their Moms and I were sitting under the magnolia tree in the yard when my friend, Jane, asked me why Doyle was limping when he ran. She said it looked as if one leg was shorter than the other one.

I was somewhat startled with her question because I had not noticed the limp. But I began to watch intently as Doyle ran toward the swing set. It did indeed appear that he was limping badly and I realized that something must be wrong. That night Johnny and I had Doyle lie down on the bed and stretch out his legs. We saw for ourselves that the left leg was indeed shorter than the right and that the left foot was smaller than the other foot. I took him to the doctor in Foley the following Friday. He examined his leg and had him walk down the hall. The doctor confirmed what we already knew concerning Doyle's left leg. One leg was shorter and his foot was smaller than the other one. Dr. Mickelsen told us that he would have to make an appointment for Doyle to see an orthopedic doctor in Mobile on Monday morning. He said he suspected that he had something with a big name called Osteochondritis. I had never heard the word and somehow got it in my mind that he suspected bone cancer. He told us that Dr. Lloyd Russell, the orthopedist, would explain the disease to us. Johnny and I spent a long worrisome two days with constant petitions sent up to the Lord. We told Doyle not to run and to stay in the house for the next two days.

We were filled with anxiety when we arrived at Dr. Russell's office in Mobile the following Monday. He examined and x-rayed Doyle's hip again and explained to us that Doyle's condition was referred to as Legg Perthes which was a degenerative disease where the growth of the bone was prohibited because the blood stopped flowing to the hip joint. I heard later that this disease usually affected boys between the ages of 6 to 12. For some reason the top of the hip joint had become inflamed and flattened out. The disease can be very painful, but Doyle never complained to me of pain in his hip. It seemed he had a high pain tolerance because he would not tell me when his ears were hurting with infection until he could no longer stand the pain. The treatment was to remove all pressure from the hip joint by not putting weight on his leg so the bone marrow would grow again. He was fitted with a brace that fit around his ankle and a shoulder strap that hooked to that leg in order to pull it up and behind him. When it was hooked he then had to use crutches in order to walk. Doyle took everything in stride and learned to almost run on his crutches. It was so hard for him to remember to hook the strap back up after he had been sitting on the ground playing at recess. After wearing the brace for 14 months which seemed like an eternity the doctor said he could finally start walking on his leg again but he was not supposed to run. When he went out to play I tried to watch him closely knowing he would forget that he must walk but he had a lot of energy and would soon start running. Eventually his leg and foot started growing once more and we began to relax again. By the time Doyle was grown he hardly limped at all and his left foot and leg had grown to almost the same size of the right one. God had seen us through an ordeal. Without the pressure on his leg the blood began flowing to his hip joint again and the marrow was restored. Our prayers had been answered and the long awaited day we had dreamed of had come to pass. Doyle's body was healed.

While Doyle could not do much to help out with the chores such as feeding the bird dogs and helping Johnny we seemed to depend more and more on Barry. He was older and stronger and I knew we called on him too much. But Johnny took them fishing and dove hunting. One day they all went to a pond in Summerdale that belonged to Calvin Childress, who was Daddy's cousin's husband. It was raining cats and dogs that day and when they did not come home for hours I really began to worry. I wondered how they could fish with the rain pouring down so hard. I had supper ready at dark and when they still had not made it home I could not imagine what had happened. I wondered if one of them had gotten sick or hurt and they could not get word to me.

Just as I decided to go look for what I knew were my three drenched and starved fishermen they came home. They called for me to come see the catch of the day. I was pretty upset with them by that time and started not to go outside. But when I saw the strings of fish they caught I knew the fish were biting good and they could not make themselves leave. We would have fish to eat for days so I calmed down and joined in the excitement.

Johnny wanted to train Barry early in life to hunt. I did not approve of some of his escapades because one night he sat Barry on the front fender of our old pick-up truck and gave him a 410 shot gun. Rabbits were very plentiful and Johnny sold what he killed to a man at the base. Johnny spotted a rabbit from the light of his headlights and told Barry to shoot the gun. The gun fired quickly throwing Barry up in the air, off the truck and onto the ground. He looked up and all he could see were the stars in the sky. He killed the rabbit and was happy because it was his first one. Johnny was so frightened he let the rabbit hunting go until Barry was older.

When Barry was 11 or 12 he was an avid collector of model airplanes. He always asked for model airplane kits for his birthday, Christmas or any other occasion when we bought gifts. He spent hours talking to his dad about the different air planes he had worked on and the planes that were flown in the wars. After supper he would spread all the delicate parts to assemble on the dinette table, find his glue and work on them until bedtime. After he finished several models he strung a wire across his bedroom and hung them on it so little hands could not reach his new inventions. When he ran out of room he set his larger planes on a night stand by his bed.

However, one day I had company and my friend just happened to have an inquisitive little boy. While we were in the kitchen visiting over coffee Stevie managed to grab one of the big planes and it broke while he played with it. The other children hurried to tell us what Stevie had done. When Barry came home from school he was furious. It happened that the child's father was Barry's teacher and he threatened to tell Steve's daddy, but I told him he was just a child and we would buy him other planes. I tried to explain that Stevie thought it was a toy. Barry packed his fragile airplanes up in a box until we moved to the new house where he had shelves to put them on.

When Twila was around two years old I let her play in the backyard with Doyle one evening. I was out there with them raking up the magnolia leaves but had my back turned away from them. All of a sudden Twila came running to me bawling her eyes out. I looked her over checking her for ants and cuts and could not figure out what was wrong with her. Then I saw a small piece of Granny Ryan's ornamental red pepper plant stuck in her hand. The peppers growing on the plants were small and attractive since they grew in so many bright colors of red, green, purple and yellow. I suppose she thought the peppers were pretty so she picked one, broke it into and then rubbed her eyes. It took quite a while to get the pepper washed from her eyes and to get her to stop crying. She was just a baby but those peppers had an indelible effect on her memory. I do not remember her ever picking the peppers again.

Another funny story happened one day when Johnny went into the wash room where our wringer washing machine and the old gas hot water heater was. Twila was about three at the time and she had followed her dad out the back door. Johnny was looking for some sort of tool while inside. I suppose Twila had watched me put a contraption in the door to hold it shut when I finished the laundry because she gently took the piece of iron from the door pushed the door too and placed the lock on the outside of the door. I always hooked it thinking it would possibly keep out the snakes, but all sorts of lizards and salamanders scared me as I entered. Barry was in the kitchen when he heard his daddy hollering and trying to tear the door down. Twila was standing in the yard screaming uncontrollably because she did not know how to open the door and thought she was in trouble. By the time Barry reached the door Johnny had beaten the bottom panel out of the door. Johnny stuck his head out the hole and Barry could tell he was mad as an old wet hen. He demanded to know who locked him in the wash room. When he found out it was Twila he told her to stop crying he was alright. From then on a piece of plywood covered the hole in the washroom door.

I was so proud to be the mother of two sons and a daughter. Before Twila was born I dreamed I had a baby girl with a head full of dark hair and olive skin. Now that I had a little blonde haired, blue eyed daughter with fair complexion she was now the light of my life and my *dream* had finally come true. It was just fine that she did not have dark hair. So goes a day in the life of three growing kids.

24
Snakes, Wild Animals and Homing Pigeons

Daddy and Barry show 2 bobcats they killed on the farm. Bobcats were a danger to our young calves.

Johnny took a picture of the snake Doyle shot but missed Doyle's head.

Johnny is pictured with the trophies he won racing homing pigeons

and on the right are pigeons he sent on races. There was no betting or money involved in the races.

Although, Johnny and I could not provide every thing our children wanted, they always had enough. The few toys they received under the Christmas tree were not much, but it was enough to make them happy because they were not used to expensive toys. We wanted so badly to make their lives happier than ours when we were children. We had big plans for them to live good moral Christian lives, be good citizens, love their country, strive for a college education and help their fellowman. We let them know we were going to work hard to give them the opportunities we did not have. However, we in return expected them to help with the farm chores without pay. Their afterschool farm chores taught them responsibility. We always tried to supply their material necessities and they respected that. When it was time for them to pay college tuition and purchase books their Daddy would load up cows in the cattle trailer and sell them at the livestock auction. We never borrowed any money for their education because we usually had crops to sell in the fall or cattle to take to the auction to pay their college expenses. Many years we lived from pay-day to pay-day, but God always graciously filled our every need.

We chose to be a family. We had a rule that unless otherwise hindered each member of our family was expected to gather at the table for supper as we sat down to eat our meals together. On Sundays, they knew we would all be attending Sunday school and worship as well as the night services and Wednesday night prayer meeting. Our activities evolved around the church. Our daily walk with the Lord was important and we always tried to let it take first place in whatever we did. Our close friends were our church friends and we cherished them and their fellowship dearly. Johnny often took the boys fishing and I planned birthday parties and let them invite friends over for the weekend. Vacations were few and far between because of finances and farm work, especially when the garden vegetables were ready to be picked, but we took weekend trips to visit their Grandpa Dyess and their cousins in Paxton, Florida. They also had cousins nearby at home and in Pensacola, Florida who came to visit. All of our children took part-time jobs when they were teenagers to help purchase their own cars and gasoline.

Living on a farm with a swamp full of wild animals behind it and ponds with snakes in them provided not only recreation, but tales of adventure to share with their own children. I often walked the back forty acres near the swamp by myself in the afternoon. The trails I walked proved to become my exercise program which was also good therapy for me when I was worried or tired from long hours of stress at work or inside all day caring for Johnny's mother the last years of her life. As I crossed the dams I would listen to the gurgling of the fresh ever-running springs that flowed constantly from the ponds to the swamp. I often quoted the verses of the 23rd Psalm as the words came to my mind. When a lone crow cawed overhead in the late afternoon sky I felt as if God was keeping watch over me as I walked. Squirrels would scatter up the trees when they saw me coming and rabbits zipped under fence rows full of briars. Occasionally I would spot a mother armadillo with her young scattering under the fence trying to make it back to the wilds and away from me. In the spring time I beheld the beauty of wild white roses that climbed the tree tops and cascaded downward. When I returned home I was ready to start supper and finish other chores. Somehow I never thought much about the wild bobcats, foxes and coyotes that were silently lurking in the undergrowth behind the wire fence that separated the walking trail from the swamp. I knew they were there because Daddy and Barry had seen them, but I suppose I did not think they would attack me during the day. Johnny had also spotted several coyotes when he was on the tractor mowing the pasture.

As soon as Doyle arrived home from college he would get his gun and fishing pole and head to the ponds to fish near the swamp. He would tease me by telling me he was going snake hunting and that would frighten me terribly because I had such a fear for any kind of snake. I realized Doyle had always had an adventurous spirit since he was three years old. One night after we had gone to bed, Johnny's birddogs began barking and taking on like I had never heard them bark before. I peeped out our bedroom window and in the moonlight saw they were both on top of the big doghouse Johnny had built. So I crept to the back door trying not to awaken Johnny or the boys. I quietly opened the back door to see if another dog was traipsing around our yard when all of a sudden I heard the shrillest scream coming from the swamp to the west of our house. That scream made me tremble with fear and uncertainty. I had goose bumps all over as I stood there wondering if there was a woman in distress down by the swamp or if it was our neighbor's teenage son playing a trick on us. I woke up Johnny and asked him to come to the door and listen for the scream and see if he could figure out what it was. When it squalled again, he told me it was a panther and hurried to put his clothes on. I did not want him to leave but he made his way to the old pickup truck and drove to the next door neighbor's house and woke him up. As they were riding the fields Johnny caught a glimpse of the panther and shot at him. The animal jumped up in the air about six feet and then ran off. Johnny never knew whether or not he killed the cat that was probably hungry and prowling around to see if he could find a chicken or two to eat. After he shot the panther he went to another neighbor's house and woke him up and the three men looked for it for a long time but never found him. The next morning I told the boys about what happened. I knew Barry understood but never dreamed Doyle was taking it all so seriously. Barry was in school so Doyle was about three years old at the time. Somehow Doyle slipped out of the house after I had warned him he was not to go out and play. When I missed him I looked out the windows just in time to see him walking on the other side of the fence toward the swamp. I was almost hysterical as I ran as fast as I could to catch up with my daring young son. I breathlessly asked him where he was going after I had warned him not to go outside. He replied in his manly little voice, "I'm going to kill mean panther."

Later after we moved into our new home I was out working in the yard. When it was time for lunch I went to the barn to leave the rake. All of a sudden I heard the weirdest noise coming from the loft. I could not imagine what the cooing sound could be. I had never heard anything to compare it to. When Johnny came home that evening I told him there was some kind of strange sound coming from the barn that frightened me. He just laughed and said, "Have you not ever heard a pigeon coo?" Well, no, I suppose I had not, but I would hear their cooing and watch these brilliant colored homing pigeons glide through the air from then on. I thought the white pigeons resembled doves of peace. From the day his friend at the base gave Johnny these amazing pigeons, with built-in instincts, they would become a big part of our lives. When these few birds began to lay eggs and hatch babies we soon had a barn loft full.

Johnny joined a pigeon club in Pensacola and began to participate in their bird races. He would hurry home from work on Friday nights, catch the birds, write their band numbers on a sheet of paper and head to Pensacola. The men then placed them in a box to load on an airplane to ship to another city. As soon as the plane reached its destination someone would release all the birds at once and they would fly home as fast as they could to their original pigeon lofts. Johnny would sit for hours watching the evening sky for a tiny speck that might be one of his racing pigeons. When the birds landed they usually went into the opening of the loft to find water and their mate, but on other days they would land in a tree or on top of a building and rest a bit. Johnny had to wait patiently knowing this delay might cause him to lose the race. It would be a happy day for Johnny if he got the first bird home and he had a chance to win the race. No one would know for sure who won until they figured the distance and speed of the bird the following Monday night.

Johnny was just a young boy living in Louisville, Kentucky, when he got his first homing pigeons that he kept in his back yard. While a lot of young boys were off looking for mischief to get into, he and some friends would put their birds in small boxes in their bicycle baskets and head out of town to a space clear of power lines to let the birds go. Then they would jump back on their bicycles and ride as fast as they could trying to reach home before the birds arrived. The birds almost always won that race. When his dad passed away and Johnny and his mother moved to Elsanor he brought a few pigeons with him on the train.

The boys and I never looked forward to Saturdays when their dad had to work overtime. It meant that one of us had to climb a ladder to the pigeon loft in the barn and sit there for hours watching for his racing pigeons to return. When one of his feathered friends finally landed on the trap door and flew into the loft we had to enter the loft, catch the bird and take the rubber band from his leg. Time was of the essence as we hurried to place the band inside his clock and turn the key that recorded the time of the bird's arrival. As the boys got older there were other Saturday activities they needed to attend so at times I would have to be the bird watcher.

One Saturday my friend, Jane, took some of the kids to Gulf Shores on a school outing. I remember that Doyle went with her and that Barry was on the tractor plowing for his dad. Just before it was time for me to climb the ladder to the loft I got a call from Jane's sister-in-law. She said that she needed to get in touch with Jane's husband, Ford, because his mother had taken a turn for the worse in the nursing home. Well, I loved Mrs. Hedden dearly so I wanted to head to Gulf Shores and look for Jane after I called the Navy base to get word to Ford to go to his mother. Johnny said he would give him the message but I found out they had carpooled with another man to work. I then called Gulf Shore's police and asked them to try to find Jane at the state park or pavilion. My hands were tied because I knew if I left and several birds came home with no one to clock them I would be fussed at. After I did what I could I went to the loft and prayed for God to keep Mrs. Hedden alive until another one of her family members arrived. It turned out that Jane got the message and went straight to the nursing home before her mother-in-law passed away. I left the loft and made it to the hospital before Mrs. Hedden passed away. Ford was late getting there because he did not have transportation. Johnny did not win the pigeon race that day. He finally bought a siren which he installed on his truck and somehow ran a wire to the pigeon door. If a pigeon landed on the drop door it would go off and let us know a pigeon had arrived. The only trouble was that our yard birds would land on the landing and activate the siren. We would rush out to the barn only to find out that it was a false alarm.

Johnny got a lot of notoriety concerning his pigeons. Journalist were always asking to interview him so they could write an article for the newspaper. A popular star from one of the local television stations came out to make a video for his evening news show on Channel 10 in Mobile. Several pigeon fanciers came over to be here when he arrived. The interview went well and they ran the 10 minute feature that week. Not long afterwards another reporter came for an interview. The day after she was here the birds were shipped to Nashville, Tennessee. I told the reporter that Johnny could not possibly win the race because he had not had time to train his birds for the two-day race. I went to church on Sunday morning knowing no one in the club had a bird back from Nashville. After Sunday school I went into the sanctuary and sat down when suddenly Johnny appeared and whispered, "I have a bird that was in the race home and no one else in the club has one." I looked at him and said, "Don't be telling falsehoods in the Lord's house." He said, "That's the Gospel truth." And so it was because he has the trophy to show for it.

When Doyle was about ten years old he and his Daddy went hunting early one cold morning in December on some property we rented. The ground was covered with frost and the land was then covered with Tung-oil trees and a lot of Tung nuts lay in the grown up brush. As they walked carrying their guns Johnny spied a large rattle snake. Doyle begged his dad to let him shoot it. Johnny hesitated thinking Doyle might miss the snake and they would be in danger but finally told him to fire away. Doyle blew the snake's head off causing his dad to call him the marksman of the family. Johnny took a picture of Doyle holding the snake but it turned out just like all the other pictures he made. He got the snake in the picture but missed Doyle's head.

I asked Doyle not to go down to the swamp looking for moccasins, but he always replied that he needed to get them out of the ponds so they could fish and if he saw one he would kill it. He took Dusty with him and that proved to be a good decision that day because Dusty no doubt saved his life.

25

Man's Best Friend

By: Doyle Ryan

"I was in the prime of my manhood when I decided to cut my way through the swamp one day to do some fishing in the creek below one of our ponds. Equipped with a machete, my .22 caliber pistol and a can of worms I began my journey. I knew the brush would be thick going in so I would take my pole from whatever nature provided upon arrival at the fishing hole. I crossed the pasture and was approaching the wood line when I noticed my sister's dog (Dusty) running across the field to join me on my excursion. While I welcomed his company, I never imagined it would be a life saving detail.

"I had fished this creek farther up stream but knew there had to be some good fishing spots downstream that no one would care to try to get to. I have always respected these areas of the swamp but didn't really adhere to the dangers due to my adventurous nature. As I cut my way through the dense foliage I apparently stuck a limb in my leg from the brush I was chopping with the machete. I did not realize I was bleeding like a stuck hog. Knee surgery had severed the nerves above the injury and left me with no feeling in my leg there. I cut one sleeve off my shirt to tightly bandage the wound and began my search for a limb to attach my fishing line to. After baiting my hook with one of the big wigglers I dug for the occasion, I was ready to fish. As I dropped my line in the water I began to back up to a stump to sit down. Just then Dusty began to bark and went into his "something is wrong" mode. He was a smart little dog and had a lot of woods sense so I turned to look and there on the stump I was about to sit on was a coiled five foot water moccasin. For the first time in my life I realized why country folk called them cottonmouths because the inside of its mouth was truly solid white. My startled reaction created a situation in which I didn't know who was more scared, me or the snake. I do not remember what happened to the pole in my hand but the gun was there before my next thought appeared. The only problem was it was way too small for this adversary.

"We spent the next half hour playing cat & mouse (or snake & idiot) chasing each other through pockets of water and leaves and woods. As it turned out the six bullets I had in the small .22 caliber pistol would only make him mad or get him moving again. Sometimes after me! It was amazing how a snake that size could blend in with the natural surroundings. I was finally able to finish him off with the machete from an overhanging limb above his refuge in the muddy mess we created.

"I really didn't think anyone would believe how big that dead cottonmouth was because I had never seen one near that size before. So, after catching a nice string of fish, I brought it out and hung it on the barbwire fence for evidence. A couple of days later my dad admitted he thought I had exaggerated the size of the snake until he saw it. My sister's dog, a mixed breed mutt, literally saved my life that day. There is no way I could have survived a bite from that huge water moccasin that far down in the woods with no way to contact anyone."

26
Defying the Laws of Nature

By: Doyle Ryan

"Dusty"

Doyle holding his pet skunk

"It was a cool autumn day and perfect for a leisurely stroll around the fields and maybe even the woods. One never knows what adventure such a trip might hold. For every uneventful day spent in the woods there was always one that would provide a unique experience. Sometimes it would be a lifetime memory. Little did I know this would be one of those days.

"It had been an unusually boring trip around the north forty so I cut through the last finger of woods between the ponds on my way back to the house. Movement caught my eye in the woods to my right. It was a small animal making its way toward me. I guessed it was not aware of my presence because every living creature in these woods was wild. I stood motionless until I realized it was a skunk. His large white stripes from head to tail identified him as a male. He appeared to be a full grown adult. What makes this unusual is that daytime sightings are rare as skunks are mostly nocturnal. My instincts were telling me to leave quickly but this would be another of those times where adventure rules. For some reason I could not resist the allure of this little fellow as he closed the gap between us to about ten feet. If I would have known then what I know now that was much too close.

At that moment he stopped and appeared to try to figure out if I was a friend or foe. In an unexplainable way we simultaneously defied the laws of nature to accept each other in an environment that makes such an agreement very improbable. For anyone who may consider this a divine experience let me suggest you not try this with a skunk. After determining I was not a threat he began to move toward me again. It was then I noticed he had an obvious injury to his hip or back leg. I wanted to help but was afraid to let him get any closer. After all, my mom tells the story of my grandfather getting kicked out of school after getting sprayed by a skunk and going on to school reeking of skunk odor. His fourth grade classmates voted for him to go home. He never returned to finish his education.

"I made the decision to leave and head back to the house. I took several quick steps and with him following in my footsteps picked up the pace so he could not keep up. As I neared the house I thought about the occupational survey test I had recently taken in school that gave me my highest grade in animal husbandry. Are you kidding? I didn't even know what that meant let alone there are jobs that relate. I would soon have a better understanding but I still don't know how they design those test questions to sum up with such accurate results. Anyway, my conscience got the best of me and I found myself headed back to the woods with a wooden cage that I had kept a variety of animals in. Upon arriving where I left him he seemed to be waiting patiently for my return. I was actually hoping he would be gone. I knew he had to turn around to spray me so I cautiously lowered the wooden cage while watching for the first sign of an about face. To my surprise he welcomed the cage and went right into the dark end of it. Now what? My mom let me have just about everything I ever brought home from these woods including raccoons, foxes, possums, gopher turtles; but a skunk?

"Knowing better than to ask her blessing I got him set up in a larger cage with food, water and a cover for the cage until he could prove harmless. Weeks passed with no sign of smell at all. Could I have possibly caught someone's pet that had the scent glands removed? We did not have many neighbors and none knew of anyone having a pet skunk. His hip healed in time and he became a normal pet. I would take him out of his cage and carry him around the yard. He even accepted my sister's dog as a playmate until the day…

"I was in my first year of college. As I hit the backdoor on my way to school one morning a smell I could only associate with a run over skunk on the road filled the air. Could it be? It was! All these weeks with no sign of a working scent gland but he sure had it working now. I guessed a stray dog or other animal appeared to be a threat to him in his cage so he used his natural defense. I had an acquaintance that had offered me a good price for my pet skunk. In fact he wanted him badly. I wanted him to have a good home so I gave in and took his money. I am not sure how that turned out but he left with him in his car."

27
To Build or Not to Build

I remember the day as if it were yesterday. I was taking a break from my work and reading a book to our eager to learn sweet little four-year-old-daughter, Twila, as I sat in the early American rocking chair Johnny bought me. When he came in the back door from work and sat down I noticed the somber look on his face and asked what was wrong? He blurted out that it was rumored that Brookley Air Force Base was on a list of bases scheduled to close and that he would soon be without a job unless we moved to Warner Robbins, Georgia or to another base somewhere in California. I sat there stunned and in shock trying to absorb what he was saying. My heart seemed to stop for a minute, but when the news began to sink in I quickly assured him I did not want to move anywhere. Our hopes and dreams for the future were right where we were. Johnny had gained a lot of experience as an aircraft mechanic while in the Air force and also on the job at Brookley. He had flown to other states to attend schooling concerning work on many different models of aircraft including the Air Force Thunder Birds and the Navy's Blue Angel jets, so it was our hope he could secure a job at the Naval Air Station in Pensacola, Florida.

I began to question Johnny concerning what we needed to do since we were ready to start construction on the house. I could tell he was devastated too, but at the time he did not have a clue what he would do, except moving away was out of the question. He had worked too hard and made too many plans to leave his beloved farm land he had acquired by the sweat of his brow.

The spot where the Little House stood was the place he and his mother had first lived when they arrived here to stay with his sister, Ruth and her family. At the time he had nothing except his daddy's tools, some pigeons and a dog named Shep that he brought from Louisville, Kentucky. Now he owned the house and land. I sat there and thought about the new house I had *dreamed* of for so long that had seemed to become such a reality. All of our hopes and *dreams* for the future would have to be put on hold until Johnny could find another job. I began to pray silently for God to help us and guide us concerning what to do. I thought about the Bible verse where Jesus said he would never leave or forsake us and how we needed Him now.

We kept our appointment with our architect, Mr. Charles Gay of Daphne, who had drawn our blueprints. While we were on our way to pick them up one day we heard on the radio that Brookley Field was definitely closing and that some of the employees would be transferred to other bases. Johnny immediately applied for a job interview at NAS. When the Personnel Director interviewed him he told him he did not have enough sick leave days built up. Johnny tried to explain to him that he had recently had surgery on his elbow that he injured on the job the Christmas Eve before and had used a lot of his sick leave. He was still on limited duty and unable to do heavy work. So I suppose the person who interviewed him figured that he was not dependable which was far from true. He was so disappointed that he was not hired. However, later on the base received orders to transfer a certain number of men from Brookley to NAS because of a new government contract the Navy had secured. We were jubilant when we found out Johnny was one of the Alabama men.

Frocks I made for Twila and Myself on my new sewing machine

Mechanics from Brookley who were transferred to the Naval Air Station heard through the grapevine that the civil service workers at NAS resented all the Alabama boys who were being transferred there because they might take their promotions. As it turned out Johnny never lost a day of work because he left Brookley after work one day and reported to NAS on limited duty the next day. He was surprised to find out that the way the Navy worked on aircraft was very antique compared to the Air Force. When they worked on the wings they had to manually hold them up. However, we were happy Johnny had a job and a future.

Our prayers had been answered. The construction of our new

home would begin on schedule. Meanwhile Johnny cultivated the soy beans and pulled out weeds that grew among them on Saturdays. I stayed busy with everyday household duties and enjoyed sewing on my new portable Singer sewing machine. By now I was making all my clothes and Twila's plus there was always a lot of mending to do. My new sewing machine sewed like a dream compared to my old reconditioned treadle model. No longer did I have to make button holes by hand like my home economics teacher taught me since this machine had a zigzag stitch. I could now make outfits that looked professional. I made several outfits for me to wear to church. Material was cheap then so I looked for material and patterns on sale. I needed a new dress to wear to Elsanor Homemaker's Christmas party at Ruth Sirmon's home so I found a pretty piece of green wool and also bought a belt kit so I could cover the belt. We dressed up for the occasion and I received a lot of compliments on my outfit and matching beads and clip-on earrings. I bought a piece of material for a new dress for Twila. The material was red with tiny yellow daisies blending in. Our little girl had straight golden blonde hair like her daddy's and it was finally beginning to grow long after I had to cut it short when she contracted impetigo so the sores in her head would heal. Life continued on as usual with many prayers being offered up that we could stretch the money and building material as we built. God had not failed us yet and I chose to believe he would come through for us now and bring our dreams to fruition.

28
A Long Awaited Dream

Our new house and barn

under construction in a soybean field

Our home after completion 1968

The year was 1967. We had lived in the "Little House" as I began to refer to it for fifteen years when we finally thought that just maybe we could afford to build the new house of our dreams. Johnny had a chance to rent another 40 acres of land from our Johnson friends in Tuscaloosa. The owner's mother had grown

Tung oil nut trees on the property and struggled to gather bags of the black crusty nuts that she sold to companies who used them to make paint. Mrs. Johnson was getting up in years. Late one evening she fell in her yard and could not get up. The neighbors across the street found her the next day covered with ants so her son knew that she could no longer live alone and take care of the land. Mrs. Johnson's son, Ivan, agreed to let Johnny farm the land if he cleared all the trees and burned them. We would pay rent later on. Johnny agreed and worked extremely hard getting the new ground cleared in order to plant another watermelon crop. One night he was burning piles of debris and almost burned his tractor up. He was pushing the tree stumps onto a burning pile of brush when his tractor became lodged on a stump in the fire. He worked as fast as he could and did everything he knew to do before the tractor caught on fire. Just when he thought he would have to abandon the tractor in the raging fire, the tractor tire backed off the big stump. It was almost midnight when Johnny decided to call it a night and come home for a few hours sleep before reporting to work early at NAS. Of course I was still up wondering what might have gone wrong and praying he was alright. Johnny was so prone to accidents, I began to think of him as "an accident waiting to happen." No matter where he was working on the farm he usually came in for dinner with some injury and blood pouring from some part of his body.

After the Johnson land was cleared Johnny planted another crop of watermelons on the land. He had a bumper crop that year but did not try to sell them to truckers, instead he pulled the watermelons and loaded them on an old truck and one of us drove Doyle and Granny Ryan up to the school house on Highway 90. At that time there was a lot of traffic on 90 because Interstate 10 had not been built and people traveled Highway 90 on vacations to Florida. We sold a lot of melons there and in Robertsdale. One of Doyle's friends stayed with him in town and we drove out to check on them often. They had finished selling most of the load one day so I drove Johnny to town to drive the big truck home. When he got to Blackwater Bridge, the old truck sputtered and refused to go any further. They were in a dangerous place but managed to get the truck off the road.

We planted soy beans on the 20 acres that joined the Johnson place. We had been able to purchase this field at a low price earlier. When Johnny was on the 3 -11 shift at NAS I went to the fields with him and poured the soy beans in the hoppers while he poured up the heavy sacks of fertilizer. Then we rushed home so I could fix us a bite to eat and fix sandwiches for his supper. After the boys became teenagers and we felt they knew the ropes of plowing and disking they carried on after they got home from school. We had a blackboard in the utility room and Johnny listed the chores he wanted done that afternoon. We tried to complete them before dark. Some evenings I drove the truck and they picked up roots from the newly plowed ground. On other afternoons we picked up broken glass that had been scattered there since people dumped garbage on the land. We always strived to leave the kid's time to do their homework and have a little free time before bedtime.

That spring we planted soy beans on the 40 acres we planned to build our future home on because we were not sure what month we would start construction. The walls of the little house were bursting at the seams and we surely needed more space for our growing brood so I was ecstatic when we received our blue prints. I could hardly contain my excitement knowing I would have a modern house with hardwood floors, two bath rooms, utility room, a larger kitchen with matching modern appliances and so much more room.

As we made plans to start construction we heard that the mayor of Elberta was taking $1000 leases for local residents who were interested in tearing down old abandoned project houses on Baron Field. The Navy base had been closed and the apartments were no longer needed. We put up one thousand dollars and signed the contract. If we got the duplex demolished and the lot cleared by the due date our money would be returned. We figured that this blessing was sent from God and thanked Him for his goodness. Johnny hitched up the trailer to his old truck and hired a local teenager to help him dismantle the building on Saturdays. Barry was only 12 years old but he was a big help, too. They would be hungry and tired when they arrived home late on Saturday nights with treasures of good fixtures, old bricks, a lot of hardwood and other good lumber that could be used during construction of the house. All of the supplies would be carefully stored in an old barn until the day they were needed.

One Saturday it was raining but Johnny went on to disassemble the project houses since he needed to finish the job. Later his brother-in-law, Biddle Howell, came from Pensacola, left his wife, Elsie and son, Michael, with me and her mother and proceeded on to Foley to help Johnny. Biddle was a big tall man and when he climbed up to the rafters that were wet from the rain he slipped and fell. Luckily they had already removed the hardwood floors so he hit the soft ground, but was still badly injured since he had fallen so far. An ambulance took him first to the hospital in Foley and later transferred him to a Pensacola hospital nearer his home.

During this time the county was in the process of paving our dirt road and it was very muddy and sloppy. Since we had not been able to get a telephone Johnny had to call our pastor and ask him to come inform us about the accident. Elsie and I put the kids in my car and made our way down the muddy road. Somehow I managed to not get stuck or slip into the ditch. We felt badly that he was suffering from a dislocated shoulder and so many bruises and soreness. We appreciated his willingness to help. I cooked food and carried it to their children since Elsie was at the hospital so much. Biddle was a foreman at NAS and they had been able to purchase a new home in Pensacola. They were glad that we were going to have a better house.

When our blue prints were completed, I could hardly believe that we would be able to construct our dream home on $13,000 dollars that Federal Land Bank agreed to loan us and the materials salvaged from the project houses. We secured a farm loan for 20 years with monthly payments of $93.56. Johnny had another ace in the hole when he decided to cut the tall pines on our land and take them to Mr. Russell's sawmill in Magnolia Springs to be sawed into different widths and lengths of lumber needed. Mr. Russell would bring us the lumber when we began building. I was beginning to believe that dreams really do come true.

29
Construction Finally Begins

We began family devotions on Christmas Eve.

First Christmas at the new house.

It was good to have a field of watermelons to sell on the roadside or to grow a small field of corn to feed our farm animals such as the hogs we raised to sell at Robertsdale Livestock Auction. As we were able to purchase more land Johnny began to plant soy beans and then rotate the fields with corn. Most of the time the price of soy beans was good, but if not, he would store them until the market price was better and then sell.

In 1966 we planted soy beans on the 40 acres we were going to build on and it looked as if we would have a good crop. However, we had to sacrifice a couple of acres and mow them down so construction on the house could begin. We used some of the profit from a good yield that fall to help with building expenses. It was one of the busiest summers of my life. Daddy and Miss Lillie came down to help get the materials ready. Since Granny Ryan had moved into her trailer they slept on a hide-a-bed in the small room she had occupied in the little house that had been turned into a living room. During the day Daddy and Barry cleaned the used bricks by scraping the old mortar off them. They would be used to build the two fireplaces. They sorted and stacked lumber that would be used to build the house. After the house was dried in and bricked by other contractors they hauled dirt to fill in the front porch and did other odd jobs until time to work on the inside of the house.

I was on the run constantly trying to decide what to cook, washing our clothes, seeing to the children's needs plus making endless trips back and forth to the construction site to pick up nails and clean up scraps of lumber left in the yard. One day when we were in the midst of our busy schedule we were advised that a hurricane was coming our way. Daddy always got upset during bad weather so he asked Johnny to take him home. We all piled in the car and made a flying trip to Paxton, Florida to spend a couple of nights. As it turned out the storm was not as bad as feared so we returned home and began to work inside the house again after it had been dried in and bricked.

One day when Johnny was at work I ran down to the new house to get Daddy for dinner. I found him standing on a ladder holding a piece of heavy plywood with the top of his head and one hand while using his other hand to nail it in place. I rebuked him for doing such a dangerous thing, but he said it needed to be nailed up. From then on I sent Barry with him. Miss Lillie and I would have supper cooked when Johnny got home from his job so Johnny and I could go down and put up paneling on the walls and hang doors. One of my jobs was to sand and varnish doors and window facings. They were looking pretty good until I tried to stain the window facing in the living room to match the dark paneling. It was late on Saturday night and all I could think about was getting home to take a warm bath and shampoo and roll my hair. Suddenly, I looked at the facing as it turned an ugly reddish color. I was tired and frustrated so I just sat down in the floor and cried.

Johnny was able to wire the house for electricity and put in the telephone jacks. When he and Daddy nailed down the hardwood on the floors, I was skeptical that it would not look good because it was old, stained and uneven. But after it was sanded and varnished, it proved to be the most beautiful hardwood I had ever seen. The loan inspector had advised us earlier that we would probably have to buy carpet which was not in our budget. He later agreed with me when he saw the beautiful sheen that the varnish brought out of the old hardwood. We worked as much as possible and tried not to hire many people if we could manage ourselves. Barry was putting insulation in the walls one hot day in the summer without gloves or a shirt on. He soon started itching so badly until I had to take him home for a bath and clean clothes. After we put up the paneling that was popular in the sixties, Johnny and I put celetex on all the ceilings. I would put glue on the back of each piece of celetex and hand it up to him and then he would staple it to the plywood in the ceiling. It was there to stay. I tried to get Johnny to make some changes to the plans such as open the garage doors to the side of the house because I knew he would fill it full of tools and supplies that everyone could see when they rode by. But he would not give in. I told everybody if we built another house we would probably need to get a divorce because we never saw eye to eye. By and by the house was finished and passed inspection and we set April 15, 1968 as moving day. I made many trips the week before taking dishes and filling cabinets and closets. I never had many closets before so everything we owned had a special place.

The one thing that concerned me was that I did not have any curtains for all the windows. My sister-in-law, Rachel, gave me a book that showed step by step directions for making pleated drapes. I read it and studied it over and over but I still did not have money to purchase material for drapes, linings and pleating tape. However, one Saturday night we were working at the house after supper and Doyle came running into the house all excited. I quickly questioned him as to what was wrong because I thought something terrible had happened because he was not supposed to ride his bike in the dark. He tried to explain that I had a call from Hammond's Grocery Store that was still having drawings. Doyle said I had a call from Mr. Walter Hammond telling me I was the winner of their weekly drawing and that I could pick up the $75.00 on Monday. There was no need to be present to win then. I knew it was God answering my prayer concerning material for drapes. I was so relieved that everyone at home was alright and also excited that now I could spend my days sewing lined pleated drapes that would open and close with a cord after we moved. We would not need blinds.

The day we moved went so smoothly with our relatives helping out. As I stripped the beds I washed the sheets for the last time on my wringer washing machine and hung them on the line to dry. We would be able to purchase my first automatic washer and dryer after we got settled in. We moved Mrs. Ryan's trailer the same day and put it beside our house so she could see the road and still be near us. I thawed out steaks that we had butchered earlier and put in the freezer and we cooked a good supper. I was still on cloud nine. It was hard to believe that my dream of owning a new home had finally materialized so I did not realize how tired I was until I went to bed with everything in its place. I was finally in the house of my dreams even if people passing could see in the windows and most of my furniture was old. Our living room would be empty except for the nice Broyhill table with eight chairs and a china cabinet we purchased at a place that was going out of business. God had again blessed our family more than we ever deserved. One of my biggest dreams had been fulfilled and I was so thankful. I had never lived in a new house with beautiful floors, new cabinets, two bathrooms and lots of closet space.

Not long after we settled down in the yellow brick house we heard through the grapevine that the 40 acres of tall timber laying next to our land line beside our new barn that Johnny had almost finished was for sale. The owner was taking bids on the property with the highest bidder receiving the right to purchase it. Then we understood that a local man who bought and stored old equipment on his property was going to make a bid and use the land for what we referred to as a junk yard. I thought, "Oh! No! Not a junk yard next to our new home we had waited so long to enjoy." Circumstances did not look good because we had just borrowed over $13,000 to build and now we were uncertain how we would raise the money if we were the highest bidder. Johnny contacted Walter Lindsay Sr. from Bay Minette who had previously sold us the 40 acres our house was built on. He told us if we were the highest bidder he would buy the land and sell it to us later. After a few months the papers were signed and the land was ours. Johnny figured that he could get the tall timber cut and make several thousand to pay on the mortgage and he was right. He had the timber cut and also sold some land he had redeemed near Daddy's place and quickly paid off the note. Later, we hired a bulldozer to clear the stumps and planted another 40 acres of watermelons. Once again God had answered our prayers in time of need and prospered us more than we ever imagined. Since we had more land to farm now the little Ferguson 20 tractor parked in the barn became too small so Johnny purchased a new larger Ferguson tractor.

Today our house is 44 years old and cannot compare with many of the beautiful new homes in the area but in 1967 it might have been ranked in the top 10 or 20 new homes of our community. Thankfully we paid our mortgage off years ago without ever missing a payment. Now the paneled walls are out of date, and the doors and columns need replacing. It seems strange that after we moved into our new house I still dream that we are back in the little house struggling to find room for visitors to sleep. Whenever I have these frequent dreams, I wake up and thank God for the house He provided for us to rear our children in. I praise Him for giving me space to enjoy our grandchildren and other visitors when they come. I will forever appreciate a warm house in winter and a cool house in summer that is free from the critters that bothered us in our first house.

Over the years we have collected a lot of stuff that we could certainly do without, but will not part with any of it. So I feel overcome at times because we have wall to wall furniture, closets that are too full and an office full of junk, but that's life. The older we get the more we cling to old things that we cannot take with us when we are gone. Whenever I ask Johnny to clean up the junk mail and throw it away, he replies that he has not read it all yet. His desk and chest is piled high with old papers. I call him a hoarder and he refers to me as a collector. After nearly 60 years of marriage we decided to let the children deal with all the old farm equipment that is rusting in the pasture and the many odds and ends that I have sitting around the house. That will be one big mile long yard sale or a dream for all these people who go to yard sales! Wow!

30
The Mustang Craze

Barry's White Mustang

The Fastback Ford Mustang

Our family was recently reminiscing about the first cars our children owned when we realized that our two sons and our daughter all drove used Mustangs when they were teenagers. Our oldest son, Barry, worked every chance he got when he was growing up. He started out helping local farmers load watermelons in the spring and hay in the fall. One summer he worked long hours on a corn and potato shed and another year he secured a job as a flagman for a construction company who was building a road at NAS. It was such a hot summer that his lips blistered and broke out in sores as he stood in the hot sun directing traffic all day. He was able to ride back and forth to work with his daddy. So he was happy when the owner of Western Auto Store, Robert Tyson, (who later became mayor of Robertsdale) hired him to work in his air conditioned store. He and Mr. Tyson's son, Neil, worked in the afternoon putting bicycles and lawn mowers together, delivering furniture and performing other jobs.

Every job Barry had no matter how small he saved most of the earnings after taking out his tithe for the church. His bank account grew even though we were unable to pay him for the work he did on the farm. Johnny and I were saving what we could for the children's college tuition and books. We gave them spending money occasionally, money for gasoline, bought their clothes and put food on the table so they never asked for anything more.

I will always remember the fall of 1971 when Barry entered Robertsdale High School as a senior. Since he needed transportation, I told him he could drive our 1968 Chevrolet Bel-Air to school so he could go to his after school job at Western Auto. His Daddy was trying to locate him a car. On that first day of school, around noon, I was involved in a terrifying accident that could have taken my life as well as Ruth's, but God was gracious. I was laid up with a big heavy cast on my broken foot, so I was not able to drive. During those six or seven weeks Barry drove the Chevy to school, then to his job and later he would come home and make chili, spaghetti or something simple for our supper. Johnny was on the 3 to 11 work shift at the time. It was a few weeks before I could hobble around on crutches and cook. I had terrible nightmares and never wanted to drive a car again. However, when the cast was removed from my broken foot several weeks later, I had no choice but to drive myself to therapy until I could walk without crutches again. The dilemma was how would Barry get to his after-school job?

Barry and his dad began shopping for a car at the used car lots in town. Barry saw a cream/white 1969 Fastback Ford Mustang with black and white interior and a 351 engine at the used car dealership. I suppose it was just what he wanted because he went to the bank, drew out his savings and the search ended. The car looked good and only had 35,000 miles on it. I cannot remember how much they wanted for the car, but Barry knew he had found his dream car. After he got the Mustang home he modified the exhaust system by taking the muffler off and replacing it with two glass packs. He thought the Mustang was cool and he wanted it to make a lot of loud noise. I always lay awake until the kids arrived home when they were out at night. I could hear the Mustang as it turned the last corner down the road and then pulled into the driveway. As soon as I heard footsteps creaking on the hardwood floor in the hall, I went to sleep. It was just a mother-thing waiting until all the chicks were safely home. His daddy slept soundly by my side because 4:30 came early on work days.

One evening after Johnny got home from work he needed to plow a field but the tractor would not start. He told Barry to take me to Pensacola to the discount parts store so I could write a check for the part so he could repair the tractor. He said the store would close within the hour so we needed to hurry. I hesitantly got into the Mustang and we took off. I felt like I was sitting on the ground and the roar from that big 351 engine was hurting my ears as Barry speedily drove east on Highway 90. The loud music on the radio was not helping my nerves either. I knew we were taking a chance going over the speed limit, but when Johnny said hurry, we fell into line. I looked over at Barry and he was feeling good as he sped down the highway. He was on a mission to beat the clock. We arrived just before closing time, bought the part, and were soon on our way home. Once home, I felt as if I had been on a ride for my life. I was so relieved to get out of that teen-age monster and that is the only memory I have of riding in it. It rode as rough as I imagine a wild Mustang horse would ride. I would take our Ford LTD over the Mustang any day. We bought the large Ford LTD after we sold the Chevy when the air conditioner went out.

Barry drove the Mustang not only during his senior year to high school, but two years to Faulkner State College, and two years to the University of South Alabama. The Ford Mustang proved to be a reliable and dependable vehicle because it never had to have any major repairs. When he received his BS in Criminology he had driven the Mustang over 100,000 miles. He eventually sold it to a local high school boy and we would see the car on the road from time to time.

After Barry graduated he continued his education at USA for another year until he received his Master's degree in Education. For transportation he repaired the Ford LTD that was our family car before Johnny wrecked it on his way to work. No one can stay young forever; boys have their sport cars, but they soon wear out and they become men with families and family vehicles. Still the memory of their first sports car lingers in their hearts.

31
The Green Machine

Doyle's Green Mustang

Our son, Doyle, approached his dad when he was a junior in high school during the 1973-74 school terms concerning his need for a car. He explained if he was going be able to hold down an after-school and summer job, he had to have some wheels. Doyle, like his older brother, Barry, had also worked part-time jobs for local farmers. He had plowed and disked with a tractor, pulled corn and picked okra. He also worked for Robert L. Berner Pecan Company bagging pecans. The kids at school teased him about working at the "Nut House." Now that Doyle wanted to look for other part-time jobs he wanted a car to drive to work, school, and on dates. After he secured a part-time job at the Western Auto Store that had been sold to James "Jack" Tyson he needed transportation. This job helped buy his gasoline, clothes and gave him spending money because by this time he was interested in dating. Johnny figured the time had come to go to Key Ford at Car City in Pensacola and start car shopping.

While they were looking around the car lot, Doyle spotted a green 1972 Ford Mustang that was everything he ever wanted in a car. Although he had some savings his dad had agreed to pay the difference of the price of the car. Johnny made an offer to the salesman. It had always been his custom to never pay the market price, but try to get the manager to lower the asking price. After bickering back and forth, the salesman told Johnny they would have to have more money than he offered. Johnny quickly informed the salesman that the deal was off and they were leaving. Doyle was so disheartened but knew not to say anything in front of the salesman. Once in the car, he let his dad know that he really wanted that car, but Johnny was determined not to pay the price listed on the Mustang. I am sure he saw how disappointed Doyle was even if he did not argue with his dad. As they were about to leave the dealership, the salesman came back over and told them they had a deal. They could have the Mustang for the bid Johnny made. Doyle was one happy teenager when he came home driving the car that we came to refer to as "The Green Machine." I was happy that Doyle's Mustang did not make as much noise as his brother's. However, to my dismay, he installed six speakers for the radio, so instead of hearing a loud motor when he turned the corner on his way home I heard the loudest rock music with words I never understood. I was surprised the neighbors did not complain because Doyle rolled his windows down. I knew that loud music was detrimental to his hearing.

The summer after Doyle got his Mustang, he and a friend worked at Gulf Shores Amusement Park. In fact, he began dating a girl who lived in Mobile that he met at Gulf Shores. He was on his way to see her the day they opened the new "Bay Bridge" spanning Mobile Bay that came to be known as the "Bay Way." The next day when the picture of the governor of Alabama cutting the ribbon came out in the newspaper with the first cars crossing the bridge, there was the green mustang on the front page.

After Doyle had owned the Mustang for a year or so, his dad drove it to his job in Pensacola one day. Johnny wanted to take it by the Ford dealer after work to get them to check out the wiring on the car. Doyle drove his dad's little yellow Datsun pick-up to school and work. Doyle was working on a term paper when I answered the phone that night. Johnny told me to get Doyle on the phone. I heard Doyle say, "Oh, no! Not my Mustang." Johnny told Doyle to come pick him up because he had wrecked his car. Shortly after Johnny passed Seminole on his way home after dark, a big eight-point deer jumped the fence and hit the car in the front end. Doyle was so devastated he forgot to ask his dad if he was hurt. He hurriedly left with a distressed look on his face. You would have though he had lost his best friend. When Doyle arrived on the scene, one of his classmates had stopped to see if he could have the deer. Johnny gladly gave it to the ambitious teenager and asked him if he could pull the car fender off the tire. He did so, and they were then able to drive it home without calling a wrecker. Doyle was very relieved when he found out the car was not totaled and could be repaired. They took the Mustang back to Key Ford and had a mach one grill and hood put on it, so from then on the car sported two sets of parking lights and a set of amber fog lights.

Doyle was soon on the road again and drove the car many miles with only minor repairs. He drove it to New Orleans to Mardi Gras and had a great time with his friend he worked with at the gulf. He also drove to De Funiak Springs, Florida, several times to visit his cousin Bo Dyess and date Maggie Davidson, who was one of Bo's classmates. The car carried him to Bay Minette where he attended Faulkner State College for two years and then on to Mobile to the University of South Alabama.

One Sunday after church and dinner our family along with the boy's girlfriends were all lounging in the den watching sports on television while Twila was outside with her horses. All of a sudden we heard a loud clanging noise and a horse's whinny. Those sounds got our immediate attention. We all jumped up bumping into each other as we headed for the back door. Doyle was ahead of everyone but kept slipping down as he ran with his socks on. When we saw that the swing set was missing, we knew something was terribly wrong. Twila had been tying her young filly, Spirit, to the swing set while she worked with her. Doyle ran to the north side of the house and saw Spirit running down the paved road dragging something behind her. We stared in horror because our first thought was that Twila had somehow gotten tangled up in Spirit's reins when she was spooked and she was being dragged. Doyle took off running to the road as fast as he could and then he saw Twila running down the road after Spirit. We all drew a deep breath of relief when we found out Twila was alright. She eventually caught Spirit and put her in the pasture. But that was not the end of the story. Doyle returned to the yard only to realize that Spirit had drug part of the swing set down the driver's side of his Mustang leaving terrible scratches on it. So back to the shop went the green machine to get the scratches removed. I was sorry that the Mustang got scratched, but so glad Twila was safe. It could have been a drastic situation.

In all, Doyle drove the car for five years and only parted with it after he married. When Doyle bought another car his dad made a deal with him to buy his green Mustang for Twila to drive to school and ball practice. Those were the days of the seventies, when Mustangs were part of the muscle car mania. I do not know much about all that, but I suppose muscle cars will always be with us. I have been told that a 1972 Ford Mustang in good condition would probably be worth approximately $80,000 today, that is if you could find one.

32
The Last of the Mustangs

| The red Mustang that took Twila to College | Twila and me on her graduation day |

Twila's Red Mustang

Having just graduated from Robertsdale High School, our daughter Twila was making plans to attend Troy State University on a Presidential Scholarship. She was very excited about setting off on the journey of higher education. She and her friend, Vicki Comer, had done well and were among the top ten graduating seniors of their class. While in high school she had been driving Doyle's old Mustang. She had worked at odd jobs during her high school years such as, gathering produce for a truck farmer, picking okra and cucumbers from our garden that her dad sold to co-workers at NAS, waitressing at Quincy's Restaurant and cashiering at Dollar General Store. Twila loved children and babysat for several of the neighbors and working women. She also saved what she could by buying and re-selling horses that needed more training and care. Her secret goal was to have her own dependable car to drive to college.

So, one Saturday during that summer, Twila and Johnny went car shopping. Her daddy, who was going to pay the difference on the car, knew a good buy when he saw one. Since he had gone with the boys when they bought their Mustangs it was now her turn. John had read an ad in the NAS paper on Friday that a used car dealer located in downtown Pensacola had a two year old Ford Mustang for sale. He hoped it would not sell before he and Twila got over there on Saturday. When they arrived they found the 1978 red Ford Mustang still on the lot. It sported black interior, chrome wheels, and low mileage. The car shone brightly in the sun. They found no dents or scratches on it and it immediately stole Twila's heart. A young college girl had owned the car and drove it to a local college until her grandfather bought her a new car for graduation.

Twila was so excited when the car salesman filled out the papers on the car and quoted a price of $4,500, plus the trade-in of the green Mustang. But, her joy quickly disappeared when her daddy said the price was $500 more than he wanted to pay, so he started bartering. Johnny made an offer of $4,000, but the salesman said his boss would not take it. They wanted the asking price. Twila's countenance dropped when she and her dad left the dealership's office and started walking back to the green Mustang in the parking lot. Her dad warned her not to say anything, so she was silent until they sat down in the car. With tears in her eyes and a pleading voice she said, "Daddy, I really want that car." Her dad responded by asking, "Where are the car keys?" The salesman had driven her green Mustang so he could tell them how much money they would allow for the trade-in value and had kept the keys.

Once back in the dealer's office to pick up the keys the owner blurted out a question to John. "Do you mean you are going to let $500 stand in the way of buying that car and making your daughter happy?" "No," John said, "You are." So, whether he felt sorry that a young girl whose future transportation lay in his hands was not going to have the car of her dreams or if God intervened, we will never know. I believe the answer was both because the boss relented by saying, "You have a deal." I only remember Twila's excitement when she arrived home. I was never allowed to accompany Johnny when he went car shopping because I would always say the wrong thing when he was wheeling and dealing. Before September came John had a friend install a CB radio in Twila's car. In those days before we ever heard of cell phones, CB radios came in handy. We calculated that if she broke down on her way to and from Troy that some kind hearted person would hear of her predicament and get a wrecker to tow her car to a garage. However, you could hear some foul conversations while traveling and listening to all that static. Johnny had a CB in his truck, too. Twila's CB name was "Tweety Bird." I was "Scrub Woman" and Johnny's was "Pigeon Man." Famous phrases were, "Come in, Tweety Bird" "Do you read me" and "Over and out."

We were up early packing the red Mustang to the gill the day we left for Troy State University in the fall. I rode up with Twila and came back with Loyce Comer who was taking her daughter, Vicki to college. Vicki would also be attending college at Troy on a scholarship. The two friends planned to room together. Once on campus, we followed Loyce because she and her husband, Ed, were both graduates of Troy State and she knew her way around campus. Of course, the girl's dorm room was upstairs on the fourth floor, so we all grabbed a load of stuff and climbed the stairs several times. We soon found out that there would be a third girl living with our girls in the tiniest room we had ever seen. Julie proved to be a very sweet girl and they all got along well, but I never understood how they had room to study. In her spare time Twila worked in the business office on campus and that helped with her gasoline and gave her spending money.

When Loyce and I left, we felt the girls would be fine and if they got homesick they could come home in the red Mustang until Vicki found the car she wanted. We always welcomed the friends they made and invited home with them. Once, the entire BSU, a group of 25, came down with them when they had engagements at different churches that weekend. I cooked supper for them on Saturday and Loyce prepared Sunday dinner for them at her house. During their senior year the girls found a house to rent and three of them split the rent money. Loyce and I visited them when the girls were in pageants and took lots of home cooked food in coolers and baked goodies. They made us sleep in their beds and they slept on two couches, but we did not feel so honored when one of their beds fell one night. Thankfully no one was hurt.

During Twila's junior and senior year of college she took the job of Youth Director at Bethel Baptist Church. Since she only attended classes four days a week during the summer, she drove home every weekend. She engaged parents to help with transportation and loaded youth in her Mustang to go bowling, picnicking on the river, to minister at other churches and youth rallies. Her faithful Mustang proved to be dependable and never broke down while traveling the highways and interstates. She carried some of the girls from the youth group to tour Troy and one of them enrolled, gained her Master's degree, met her husband and settled down in the area.

Twila enjoyed playing softball since playing in the little leagues at Garrett Park when she was in seventh grade, so she joined a team at Troy. Just before she and Vicki graduated, Twila injured her ankle when she slid in home plate during a game at Troy. Her foot jammed against the base and all the ligaments and tendons in her ankle were torn. Although she had to use crutches, she vowed she would not use them to cross the gym and long stage at Troy to receive her diploma. That walk proved to be the most painful walk of her life. Even though she was smiling; I knew she was in a lot of pain. She paid for that mistake for months to come. We rode up in our little Datsun pickup truck. When we left the back of the truck was piled high with all of the stuff Twila had accumulated. Johnny loaded the vacuum first so we had to sweep the carpets the best we could. The water was turned off when their roommate, Brenda, went to get her deposit back and we had not finished cleaning the bathroom. Her Granny's couch, a rocking chair, vacuum cleaner and all sorts of stuff was tied on back. We looked like the Beverly Hillbillies going down the road followed by a red Mustang with plush animals looking out the windows in tow. As soon as we made it home Twila began looking for a job. She had to find a job where she could use crutches and sit a lot so she was fortunate to locate a job at Kaiser Aluminum in Bay Minette. Her red Mustang would always be her favorite car. Over the years it served her well.

33

Going into the Hog Business

A big litter of piglets

Twila feeding two runt pigs with bottle

Johnny started raising hogs when we lived in the little house. He bought some brood sows from my brother, Bernard and hauled them home in his pick-up truck from his farm in Florida. They produced large litters of piglets. A problem sometimes occurred after he put up an electric fence in order to keep them contained in the pasture. Sometimes a weed would short out the fence and the hogs ventured out to find other grass and Granny Ryan's flowers in the yard. They usually got out of the pen after Johnny left for work early in the morning. I would see the boys off to school and then discover the hogs were missing from the corn field where they had been feasting on leftover grain. I was never good at chasing hogs. The problem was that I could not get them to go where I wanted them to go because they chose to scatter. I found out that it was better to get some feed in a bucket and try to lead them back to the pen after I had removed the weeds from the electric fence and got it working again. I would get just close enough for them to smell the feed and then try to lure them to follow me. I would be terrified that I could not outrun them when they discovered I had a treat for their breakfast. I did a lot of praying that I could get the hogs up and get back in the house before Twila woke up. One night after we arrived home from church Johnny went to check on the sows and the boys went with him. They found that the sow was giving birth to a large litter of pigs at that very moment. The boys got their first lesson regarding "The birds and the bees" or rather "The sows and the pigs."

Johnny asked me to water the hogs around noon time, so one day I hurriedly drew up two buckets of water and carried them to the fence. I thought I could pour the water over without spattering it on the electric fence. How wrong I was. When the water hit the electric fence and the electricity zipped through my body I screamed. From then on I turned off the fence for a few minutes before I poured the water over to the thirsty hogs. There were many other tales concerning the shock the fence gave to other family members. When we moved to our new house, much to my displeasure Johnny built a hog pen in the back field behind the house. One of the sows had a big litter of pigs and two of them were runts. The bigger pigs always got to nurse first and would not let the runts have a turn. So Twila took it upon herself to mother the two little starving pigs. She would crawl in the pen with the mama sow and the piglets and pet all of them. There was something about her that made the hogs gentle when she was around them. It has always been her nature to save the underdogs of any sort of animal or chickens. She fixed powdered milk in bottles and fed them before she went to school. The little boogers seemed to know exactly when it was time for her to arrive home from school as they would go out to meet her when she stepped off the bus. Earlier I would hear them grunting at the back door when it was almost time for the bus to come. Twila raised these two runts as her pets and became very upset when her daddy sold them to a man he worked with who later butchered them.

Johnny brought her baby rabbits that he found without their mama when he was plowing. She fed the young rabbits with an eye dropper until they were old enough to munch on lettuce and other green stuff. She kept them in a box in the garage, but they all died when Barry painted stripes on his car one night and the paint fumes overcame them. Barry's little sister was pretty upset at him when she found them sick that evening and dead the next morning.

Those young years passed by so quickly. I would stop and ponder how fast time was moving. By the time Twila was in third grade, I had resigned to the fact that she was not going to be a prim little lady, but a daring tomboy like her daddy. However, she was always happy and appreciative when I made her a new Sunday dress or cute outfit to wear to school. However, she disliked me rolling her long straight blonde hair on Saturdays because pony-tails or leaving it straight was her preference. When Twila was seven there was a lady in our church who offered to give piano lessons to the young boys and girls. Twila wanted to participate because her friends would be learning how to play piano. We bought an older piano for $50.00 and she began practicing with my encouragement. The only problem was the practice time took away from the time she wanted to spend riding and caring for her pony and playing softball with Doyle. The newness of learning to play the piano was beginning to wear off, but I insisted she stick with it because I had a dream of her playing for worship services someday. My dream really came true years later.

34
For the Love of Horses

| Twila riding Pee Wee her first pony | Her Chocolate Colored Welch Pony |

A Little Girl's Dream

When the first little Shetland pony arrived at our farm in Elsanor, he became part of the family. He definitely was loved and received a lot of special attention from our daughter, Twila. She never complained about the responsibility of feeding, grooming or training her new found friend. The following year after she learned to ride and care for her little pony, she started first grade. Before Twila left to board the school bus in the morning she ran to the pony pasture to give Pee-Wee some feed. Her first thought after arriving home in the evening was of her pony. But there were rules during the next few years that she gladly adhered to: if she had any homework, she would finish it before riding her pony or playing with her dog. She had the desire to learn and make good grades so everything fell into place except she was a little late with her nightly assigned kitchen chores sometimes.

From the time she was three years old, our daughter had a fascination for horses. I could not understand where this fascination came from, because I had no desire to even pet such a huge unpredictable animal. Her daddy had never shown much interest in horses either, except when he was growing up. At times he and his friends had stood at the rail and watched the horse races in the Kentucky Derby at Church Hill Downs when he lived in Louisville.

When Twila was born, I thought she would be like me and want to learn the traditional ways of housekeeping, sewing and embroidering. However, this never happened. When I was growing up, I was not interested in following my three brothers around and participating in their boyish adventures. But Twila enjoyed outdoor activities and being a tomboy like her brothers. I had to accept the fact that my daughter would not be a carbon copy of me and realize that was a good thing because she would be more adventurous.

By the time she was three I searched for storybooks about horses and read them over and over to her at naptime until she memorized the words on the pages even though she had not yet learned to read. Some of Twila's favorite books were: *Misty, Star of Wild Horse Canyon, Flicka*, and *Little Black Goes to the Circus*.

When she was four, Twila and her brother, Doyle, received life-like plastic horses and colts under the Christmas tree. The horses came with saddles so they took care of them until the next Christmas when Twila found Jane West, a life-like cowgirl doll with a complete wardrobe, underneath the tree. Jane West was similar to her brother, Doyle's, cowboy Johnny West and Indian Tonto with movable parts and cowboy gear. All three of them fit in the saddles on the horses and came with their own guns and gear. Twila still has Jane West in the original box it came in.

I had not given up on my daughter acting lady-like so each year she still received a doll and things I thought little girls should have to play with. One Christmas my friend and I shopped for just the right doll for our girls. Santa brought both of them a pretty life size doll named "Baby Boo." Baby Boo did all sorts of things such as drink from a bottle and suck a pacifier. She also came with extra diapers and baby clothes. But on Christmas morning when I looked in on Twila and Doyle playing with their new toys on the living room floor there sat Twila with the brown baby colt in her hands completely ignoring her new baby doll sitting in its highchair.

Before Twila reached her fifth birthday she was begging her Dad to buy her a Shetland pony. She watched all the television horse shows, such as "Flicka" and "The Lone Ranger," while wearing the hand-me-down cowboy suit (turned cowgirl) that we bought for her brother, Barry, years before in Oklahoma. With her holster and six-shooter strapped to her side she dressed up in her boots and cowgirl hat. After we moved into our newly constructed home I warned her not to wear the boots in the rooms with hardwood floors. Money was tight and I wondered where we would find a pony we could afford, but one day Uncle Horace Shumock came by to visit us on his way back to Mississippi from the Robertsdale Cattle Auction. Johnny mentioned that he was looking for a Shetland pony for Twila and Uncle Horace told him he had a pony he would sell him.

Early the next Saturday Johnny put the cattle bars on the sides of our pick-up truck and the five of us piled in the cab and headed for Moss Point, Mississippi. Aunt Ola cooked a wonderful dinner for us and we enjoyed visiting with them. Twila was anxious for Uncle Horace to finish dinner and get Pee-Wee out of his pasture. He hooked him up to a little short two-wheeled buggy with a seat large enough for two people to ride in. He rode her up and down the dirt roads by his spacious farm in Big Point making Twila one ecstatic child. We knew she had found her Shetland pony so we brought Pee-Wee home to the new pony pasture and stable. The tack that came with the pony included a diamond-shaped studded bridle and a black and red saddle trimmed in rhinestones with a shiny chrome saddle horn. Pee-Wee was content having so much attention as her new owner brushed, petted, and rode him. Johnny drove a big stake in the ground and tied a rope to Pee-Wee and Twila rode around in a circle like the ponies she had ridden at the fair until she was comfortable riding him. Uncle Horace brought the buggy to us on his next trip to Robertsdale.

I began planning Twila's fifth birthday party by inviting ten of her friends from church. Then I decorated the two-car garage with crepe paper and balloons. I asked her older cousin, Olivia, if she would ride the kids around the yard with Pee-Wee pulling the buggy during the party. Gentle and tame, Pee-Wee never once acted up during the entire evening.

One Sunday evening after saddling up Pee-Wee, Johnny and I rode ahead of her around the wooded trails in the truck while she rode the little Shetland pony behind us. All of a sudden Johnny started going faster and Pee-Wee took off running behind. Twila was not expecting the pony to take off so fast so she bounced off the saddle. We were so frightened when we looked back and saw Twila on the ground. Thankfully, much to our relief she was not injured. Pee-Wee just stopped, stood there and looked at us as if he was wondering what all the fuss was about. Therefore, a little girl's dream of owning her very own pony was fulfilled.

35
The Chocolate Colored Pony

~~~~~~~~~~~~~

Suddenly, it appeared to us Twila had out-grown Pee-Wee, and we must start looking for a larger Welch pony. One Saturday, she saw an ad in the local newspaper advertising one for sale. We called the telephone number and spoke with the owners. Twila begged her Dad to take her to Foley to look at the Welch pony before someone bought him.

When she saw him in the pasture, she immediately fell in love with the dark brown Welch pony with a high thick mane. The owners let her ride him and he proved to be gentle, so Johnny made a deal and loaded up the pony in the back of the pick-up truck with wood cattle rails attached to the sides. On the way home, we talked about a name for the new pony. She decided since his coat was dark like chocolate she would call him Cocoa. Although Twila had been sad to say good-bye to Pee-Wee, the new excitement of having Cocoa made up for the loss. Our daughter spent many happy hours riding Cocoa in the fields and on trails of the back forty of the farm.

One day Twila decided to see how fast Cocoa could run and did a test run from our barn gate down through the field to the fence in front of our neighbor's house. I was cooking supper when the phone rang and my elderly neighbor asked me if Twila's pony was running away with her. I hurried outside and found Twila dismounting so she could put him in the pasture. When I asked her if the pony ran away with her, she replied, "I was just seeing how fast he could go and doing my trick of standing up in the stirrups." Relieved, I cautioned her to be careful and returned to the kitchen.

After having Cocoa for some time, Twila came home from church at Bethel one night and informed us she had volunteered Cocoa to stand in place and represent a donkey at the live Christmas nativity scene. Her daddy thought that was a neat idea and promised he would get the pony to the church. Since the church was on a busy highway and it would be late Saturday evening, I was not so sure about their plan. Twila asked to ride Cocoa on the highway right-of-way the two miles to church. Her daddy followed driving the truck on the highway at a slow speed while keeping an eye on her. I prayed for safety as they ventured out on a little girl's dream. As Twila stood by portraying one of the angelic hosts, Cocoa turned out to be the perfect stand-in donkey such as the one Mary rode to Bethlehem.

36
Shatata

Johnny riding Shatata on the fourth of July

When Twila approached her dad about buying her a full grown horse he questioned her about selling Cocoa since she was then in Jr. High School. Although she was very attached to the Welch pony, she realized she needed a regular size horse. She also knew Cocoa would make some kid a good pony. So, the next day, Johnny went to work at the Naval Air Station and asked one of his fellow workers, Roy Jones, Sr., who had several kids, if he wanted to buy a pony. He said he did and would be over to get him that afternoon. When they came Twila was practicing softball with her team at Garrett Park that evening. Later she came home and saw the gate to the pony pasture open. She rushed in the house and told her dad and brothers that Cocoa was out of his pen and she needed help finding him. When her daddy told her he sold Cocoa to Mr. Jones in exchange for him doing some electrical wiring on Doyle's car, she burst into tears because she had not had a chance to say goodbye.

Later, Johnny bought her a horse from her cousin, Olivia, who had trained him well, yet I could not get over how tall he was for such a petite girl. Now that she had Shatata to ride she got over missing Cocoa so much. Almost every day after school and on weekends, Twila saddled up Shatata and with Dusty in tow they trotted off for adventures in the woods and around the ponds. Other members of the family envied Twila's enthusiasm of riding so they decided to mount up for rides as well. One year as the family celebrated the 4th of July, Twila's Dad took his first ride on Shatata proudly carrying the American flag around the yard. Shatata was a gentle horse except for the time when Twila was riding him down the road and a neighbor blew his car horn waving at her as they passed and it frightened him.

She proudly rode Shatata in the RHS Homecoming Parade that fall. Not long after that day, Johnny was talking to A. C. Martin at work. Mr. Martin asked Johnny if he wanted to buy a registered quarter horse. We went over to look at the beautiful brindle colored horse named "Taffy." The problem though was that Mr. Martin's grown son had some trouble mounting the high spirited horse, but we knew we wanted Taffy because in a few months she would give birth to a foal that was from a famous bloodline and could be registered. I suppose Roy Jones, Jr. (the boxer) enjoyed riding Cocoa when he was young, but Twila's *dream* and passion of owning a registered quarter house was unfolding as the months went by with Taffy in the pasture.

37
The Special Bond of Spirit

Taffy and her new foal Spirit

Twila feeding Spirit a carrot

Twila riding Spirit after school

Training Jazz when she was in college

It was an ordinary spring school day in early April of 1977. As usual I was rushing around checking to be sure the kids ate a good breakfast, had plenty of lunch and snack money, and remembered to take their books. Barry had left early for classes at University of South Alabama without any fanfare, but I still had to rush his brother

142

to get out of the shower and hurry through the morning routine before he left for classes at Faulkner State.

We had been looking out the door the first thing every morning for several days to see if the registered quarter horse's foal had been born during the night but we were running a little late this morning. Finally Doyle hurried out to get in his car to leave for Faulkner. He quickly returned and yelled for Twila, to hurry and come see what was in the pasture before she caught the school bus. Twila excitedly flew out the door to the pasture with me following behind in my housecoat and house shoes to see Taffy's long expected foal.

We stood there gazing at a perfect little reproduction of Taffy standing by its mother. Twila was so excited she could hardly contain herself. She asked me if she could please stay home from school that day. She never wanted to miss school and had even begged to go when she was feverish because she liked school and did not want to get behind in her homework. I assured her the foal would be fine and would be here when she got home. After looking the baby filly over for a few minutes, Twila ran back to get her books and reluctantly left on the bus. She was so thrilled to be able to share her good news with her friends. She was excited to be able to tell everyone about the beautiful newborn filly that was born during the night.

Since her daddy wanted to get the papers in the mail to register the foal, Twila had to choose a name for her. Twila named the foal, "Twila's Leo Spirit," but decided to call her Spirit. Leo was a name from the horse's bloodline. It was not long before she was leading the filly around the yard and teaching her to obey commands. Her dream and passion now was to train Spirit so she could ride her in horseshows. She dreamed that someday she would be able ride Spirit in barrel racing and pole bending competition.

One day I heard the strangest clanging sound and went out to see what was happening. I found out the noise was a bunch of tin cans tied together with strings and placed across Spirit's back. I asked my daughter why she was doing that and she replied that she had to get the six month old horse familiar to noise so if she took her to horseshows she would not be skittish. I began to realize that apples and carrots were constantly disappearing from the refrigerator. I found out why one day when I saw Spirit eating her treat out of Twila's hand after her obedience training lesson. Spirit turned out to be a horse with a lot of speed. She would get her exercise by running around in the pasture. One day she was running so fast that she ran into the barbed wire fence and cut a big gash in her leg making it necessary to take her to the veterinarian. Twila had the responsibility of applying salve and doctoring her each day until her wound healed.

As much as Twila enjoyed playing softball on the school team and being co-editor of the school yearbook, they all took backseat to her love of horses. She talked about horses, drew pencil drawings of them and read books on how to care for them. She went to see the Lipizzan stallions in Mobile and the Clydesdale horses when they came to town. For Christmas she asked for a new cowgirl vest, hat, boots, saddle and horse blankets or new halters. She seldom asked for jewelry, but she liked stuffed animals, so I often surprised her with a stuffed animal for Christmas.

When Spirit was old enough for her to ride, Twila started training her to round up the cows and move them out of the green winter pasture when her daddy was working. When the cows saw her and Spirit coming with Dusty keeping pace by their side, the cows would begin walking toward the gate. Whenever she started saddling Spirit, Dusty knew he was going to get his exercise by tagging along. We felt like Spirit also needed a little professional training so we took her to a professional trainer for a few weeks. I had finally accepted the fact that my daughter was the happiest when she was working with her horses and training Spirit for the day she could ride her in horse shows. When Spirit was over two years old Johnny set up barrels and poles in the pasture so she could practice barrel racing and pole bending. We had a good friend who trimmed the horse's hooves and he encouraged Twila by showing her how to practice for competition.

Her biggest thrill of horseback riding came early on Saturday mornings when she joined her cousin, Olivia, who lived down Cowpen Creek Road. Twila's dad would load Spirit up in the trailer and take her to meet her cousin at 5:30 in the morning for their day's adventure. They would ride through the woods and trails and spot all sorts of wildlife such as deer, foxes and squirrels. One day they were terribly frightened when they saw a large rattlesnake coiled beside their path. The horses were close beside the snake before they saw it. The horses took off running at such a rapid speed that Twila's cowgirl hat flew off her head. They were so thankful the poisonous snake did not strike one of the horses so the hat became unimportant and was never recovered. The days were relaxing and a time of fun, especially when they stopped by the creek to eat their lunch, splash in the water and water the horses.

Finally the long awaited night arrived when Twila and Spirit participated at their first horse show in Foley. Johnny and Twila loaded the horse in his cattle trailer and I went along to watch the event. For her first time in competition she did pretty well. She won some events which gave her the satisfaction of knowing she had done her best. Later she entered competition in Bay Minette, but before I realized it, Twila had graduated from high school and headed off to college. It was a sad time for all of us because Spirit and Dusty missed her so. I could only go to the fence and talk to Spirit and take Dusty with me on my afternoon walks in the back woods of the pasture.

Occasionally, Twila came home from college to visit, but since she was so busy with other activities she rode Spirit less and less. Then a strange thing happened. One weekend she arrived home before dark on Friday evening, saddled up Spirit and headed for the woods. In a few minutes she was back. I went to see what was wrong and found Twila putting Spirit back in the pasture. Her eyes were so swollen and red until she could hardly see. In time we had to face reality. Twila's immune system had changed since she had been away at college and she had become allergic to her horse. As time passed and her allergic reaction to horses did not subside but only worsened, we had no other choice than to sell her beloved Spirit that had brought her so much joy.

A young girl in Mobile County and her parents came over to check Spirit out. The girl climbed up on Spirit, saw how gentle, yet strong she was and knew immediately that she wanted the horse. We said our goodbyes to the horse that had fulfilled our daughter's passion and dreams. We all wished the young girl well. I never knew if Twila shed any tears, but I sure felt like crying. They later wrote us to let us know how happy they were to have Spirit and that she had won in different categories in horse shows all over the Southeast. Spirit had made two young girls with a passion for riding and competing very happy and we have always kept her gentle spirit alive with happy memories. No one can tell me animals cannot feel affection and a special bond with those who care for them because I witnessed that bond between Twila and Spirit. The golden taffy colored horse with flowing black mane and tail was the horse our daughter had always dreamed of owning.

Twila enjoyed riding so many horses that it is hard to remember all of their names. Johnny bought a white horse named Bernie who ran away with one of Twila's cousins who was visiting from North Alabama. Her mother and I stood in the yard and prayed that the horse would not throw Lee Ann because she was running so fast and we knew she would be hurt badly. Twila would ride Bernie bareback because she had such a smooth gait. She was a very long, tall horse. Once Twila and her friends wanted to see how many people would fit on Bernie. Four of them fit on her back with plenty of rump room to spare. One gentle horse we owned was named Billie. She was Jasmine's (Jazz's) mother. After Jasmine "Jazz" was born Twila spent a lot of time training her too. She was gentle and a fine looking horse but there came a time when we had to sell her also. We found Billie dead in the pasture one morning so we called the vet to come do an autopsy. He believed Billie ruptured an intestine which sometimes happens when a horse rolls on the ground. Another horse, Dan, was on the wild side to say the least. He would jump the fence of the cattle corral. We decided to sell him as no one was able to ride him. Johnny and Barry had trouble getting him to go up into the trailer. He reared up when they pulled at the ropes and then fell over backward. I thought he was dead, but he got up. Johnny eventually called a professional who knew how to load agitated horses. He knew how to get the horse into the trailer. Twila bought and sold many horses in order to make money to save for the purchase of a car.

One cold morning after Johnny had retired he sat around the fire taking care of some correspondence when it suddenly occurred to him that there might be ice in Jazz's water trough. When he got to the pasture he was shocked to discover she had barbed wire tangled around her leg and it was bleeding profusely. He called the vet who came immediately and got the bleeding stopped. The young mare was shaking from losing so much blood and could hardly stand up. Her leg was in such bad shape the vet advised Johnny that in order to save her leg he would have to take very good care of her.

Johnny found horse blankets to wrap around Jazz and fixed her a bed of hay in her stall. Everyday for about 10 days he had her stand in a bucket of warm salt water and then doctored and bandaged her leg. We did not write Twila that the mare she had raised from a foal might not make it if her leg became gangrenous. Johnny did just as the vet had ordered until Jazz recovered. By the time Twila got home from college, only the scar was visible. Jazz had made a full recovery and although she limped a little for awhile she soon overcame that. I was glad Johnny was home every day in order to doctor the horse because I had to go to work and would not have been any help because I never got past being afraid of the horses even though most of them were gentle in nature. We eventually sold all the horses. So ended an era of buying, raising, selling and riding horses.

In June of 1984 Twila and her friend Vickie graduated from college. Twila came home to stay until she decided what the next step in her life would be. She soon found a job with Kaiser Aluminum in Bay Minette. Although she worked fulltime she also took a part-time job at Bethel Baptist Church as Youth Director to fulfill her dream of making a difference in the lives of young people.

38
The Life of a Country Girl

~~~~~~~~~~~~~~~~~~~

By: Twila Ryan Bilon

A country girl's life is one of hard work, adventure, fun, and just living and learning about life in general. She is more than familiar with the ways of shelling, snapping, shucking, and silking the homegrown vegetables. She knows what sweat is. She also knows what freezing hands feel like. A country girl knows what it's like to walk barefoot in the freshly plowed fields feeling the cool dirt swish between her toes and throw dirt clods at imaginary targets. She digs "fox holes" with her brother as they pretend they are soldiers in the thick of battle. She picks berries and makes "Indian war paint" with her best girlfriend; then they play the part after streaking their faces with the purple stuff and putting pigeon feathers in their hair. She loves to watch and catch lightening bugs as the night sky descends. She and her friend are expert bakers in the art of mud-pie making. She is often seen romping the farm with her dog or riding her horse across the field and into the woods. She loves being outside, breathing the country air and experiencing the beauty and wonder of nature God has placed around her. She loves cool mornings in the fall, hot afternoons in the summer, and the fresh, crystal clear days of springtime. On a cold winter day, she warms by the fire in the wood burning fireplace as she watches the flames dance. She picks wildflowers in the fields, searches for four leafed clovers, and looks on in wonder as God paints the sky with a beautiful sunset after another fulfilling day in the country. She thanks God for friends, family, and the little things of life that make life good. Life is good. Life is very, very good.

Lightening Bugs

I saw a quick flash. What was that? I looked, unblinkingly, in the same location and saw the flash again. I moved closer. This time the flashing light was in a different area. I ran to get my brother, Doyle. "Come quick," I said. "There's flashing light things in the air." He grabbed a jar and lid, running out the door. I followed in my brother's footsteps, admiring my hero as he always seemed to know the answers. He never let on if I was a bother as I always wanted to be involved in whatever he was doing. Outside in the yard, we looked intently into the settling almost night sky watching in amazement a light show like no other. "Lightening bugs," he quietly told me. Wow, so that's what they are, I thought. He ran across the yard and captured one in the jar. Returning, he handed his little sister the jar. I watched in wonder as the tiny insect blinked its light at me. Throughout my life I would always remember this special moment with my brother in God's magnificent world.

39
If Only I Could have Stayed

Miss Lillie and Daddy stand in front of the Little House.

A few years after Daddy and Miss Lillie came to stay with us so Daddy could help us build our house Miss Lillie was diagnosed with cancer of the mouth. The doctor that made the diagnosis said the cancer probably occurred from years of snuff dipping. Her doctor advised her to stop the snuff and sent her to Pensacola for treatments. Since I lived closer to Pensacola, I volunteered to take her for the treatments if she would stay with us. Meanwhile the week before Johnny was to pick her up my dentist pulled one of my jaw teeth and I had what was referred to as a dry socket. I was in so much pain with that hole in my jaw until the dentist had to pack it with medication every day. I would drive to Foley to the dentist twenty miles away and get my jaw packed and then rush home to pick up Miss Lillie and head for Pensacola. It was a painful time in my life trying to keep up with the appointments, get Johnny off to work and the kids off to school plus keep the family fed and the housework done. Miss Lillie helped me when she could but I tried to get her to rest. She was just so restless if she was not doing something but she did enjoy watching her stories on television with Granny Ryan.

Eventually the doctor reported that the cancer in her mouth was in remission. Miss Lillie got along good and was happy to get home after the ordeal of cancer treatments. The problem was getting her to quit dipping snuff. She never got nauseated after treatments and felt better than I did before the dry socket got better. She seemed to be in fairly good health for a few years after that. She stayed busy helping Daddy with his gardening and working at their vegetable stand in the summer. We visited them often and she always had plenty of food cooked except the banana pudding. Since Barry liked banana pudding she always had the bananas and vanilla wafers ready for me to make the dessert.

In the fall of 1975 Ethel called me one day to let me know that Miss Lillie had been in the hospital with congestive heart failure and that she may not have long to live. We took the kids and went up to see what we could do to help that weekend. She was in the bed most of the time and could not eat much but I tried to cook her some chicken and dumplings and other things I thought she would eat. After I had cleaned the house and did what I could it was time for us to leave for home on Sunday evening. The kids all had to start school the next day and I still had to hem Barry's pants and buy a few school supplies. As we were preparing to leave Miss Lillie called me to her bed and pleaded with me to stay with her. I held her hand and told her I would gladly stay but I had to see that the kids got started in school. Johnny had to work and Granny Ryan's leg was so crippled she could hardly get around with one crutch in her trailer. So I felt I had no choice. Ethel said she would send them food and check on her every day. Bernard tried to find her son but to no avail. The Army could not tell us if he was dead or alive. I left for home with a heavy heart never dreaming what the next day would bring.

40

Two Miles from Home

I t was a Monday morning in September, 1971. The house was abuzz with activity as our three children readied themselves for their first day of school. I was up early preparing their breakfast. Barry and Twila would eat the bacon and eggs I scrambled but Doyle usually stuck by his favorite toast and homemade blackberry jelly. Barry was entering the twelfth grade and Doyle the ninth grade at Robertsdale High School while Twila was a fourth grade student at Elsanor Elementary School. Barry drove our family car that day so he would have a way to get to his job at Western Auto. Doyle still rode the school bus so he could talk with his friends.

After they left I began gathering the laundry and tackled the housework. I spoiled my kids by not giving them morning chores so there were beds to be made and hardwood floors to be dust mopped. After dinner I would get busy peeling and canning the bushel of Bartlett pears a friend had given us. I never wanted anything to go to waste plus we enjoyed pear salad made out of these delicious white pear halves. I had just finished eating my lunch when Ruth stopped by to see if I wanted to ride to town with her. I quickly checked my supply of sugar and told her I did indeed need to go with her to buy some sugar. I had wanted to take a ride in her new Oldsmobile they had just purchased, so I quickly dressed and off we went in a drizzling rain. We had turned on Highway 90 when I began writing a quick grocery list. Suddenly I heard Ruth in an alarming voice say, "He is going to hit us." I looked up just in time to see a car headed straight toward us. That was the last thing I remember until I woke up in the emergency room at South Baldwin Hospital.

We were not wearing seat belts and I hit the windshield on the passenger side. Ruth's windshield was broken leaving glass in her face and also internal injuries caused by the steering wheel. I was thrown to the floorboard and neighbors who appeared to help pulled me up and took me out of the car. Ruth had landed on my side of the car so they put me in the back seat. They said I was bleeding profusely from the mouth and nose with contusions and bruises all over my face. I also had a broken foot and a concussion. Ruth's face required stitches so she was put to sleep. We were in a room together in the hospital and that is where we stayed for several days with our families constantly coming and going. My nerves were shattered and I later became depressed as I lay on the couch day after day trying to read or watch T. V. as I tried to get my mind off the crash. I thought perhaps if I could have found a way to stay with Miss Lillie I would not be laying on the couch unable to cook and clean for my family. I stared out the den window at the spiders in the windows I planned to wash as soon as school started when the weather was cooler. However, I thanked God over and over for letting me live so I could take care of my family and hopefully see my children graduate from school and perhaps college and the birth of grandchildren. The church ladies brought food and helped out for a couple of weeks until I could stand on crutches for awhile. Johnny was so busy getting his corn dried and pulling weeds from the soybeans that he did not have time to do much in the house. While I still had the cast on my foot and leg we received a call that Miss Lillie had passed away in her sleep on a Sunday afternoon in September. Daddy was devastated since he had already lost two wives and now his third one was gone. No doubt, he knew then that he would spend the rest of his life in loneliness. Miss Lillie had been content living in the cabin in the woods and finding a family who cared.

I was able to make the trip to her funeral still wearing the heavy cast. We were her kids and grandkids and we would take care of her funeral expenses that insurance did not cover. We made a good crop of corn that year and the soybeans received a lot of rain that made them grow and produce. So with all the other problems and sadness it was good to know that our dreams of a good harvest would materialize.

41
Dropped in My Lap

Jeanette is pictured in the new office at Elsanor School on "Secretary Day."

At right Joanna Dyess, member of Elsanor PTA presents Jeanette with retirement gifts at Elsanor's Field Day.

In 1976 when Barry was a student at University of South Alabama, Doyle was taking classes at Faulkner State Community College and Twila had just completed the ninth grade at Robertsdale High School, I had a serious decision to make. I had been procrastinating concerning surgery that the doctor said I needed. Some days I was in so much pain that I had to give in and go to bed. During that summer I made the decision to have the surgery I had been putting off because I was so paranoid. Mama died five days after she had female surgery in 1950 and I also knew of other young women who had not recovered after surgery. My gynecologist, Dr. R. E. Abel assured me that operation procedures had improved tremendously since 1950, so I finally received peace about having surgery. The surgery went fine and I was home in a few days. The only setback happened a few days after I came home from the hospital. My legs started hurting because my hormone tablets needed adjusting. Dr. Abel prescribed medication to relax me which I took on an empty stomach. I felt strange and could not eat that night so I took another one. I had such a reaction that Johnny had to take me back to the hospital at 3:00 am. Twila took good care of me and at the same time picked the extra okra and garden vegetables for her daddy to sell to fellow workers at NAS. She also made extra money by baby-sitting that year. Western Auto Store was sold to another Mr. Tyson (no relation to first owner) and Doyle secured a job there after Barry moved to Mobile.

When the boys needed tuition and book money for college, Johnny would load up cattle and take them to the thriving livestock auction in Robertsdale. The boys still needed extra money for gasoline and other expenses. Twila, who at that time, was in high school began wanting to shop for her clothes that I did not feel up to sewing, so I began to realize that I needed a job in order to help the kids. Six weeks later I began to feel better so I shared my need for a job with my good friend who was a teacher at our local school. I coveted her prayers since I did not have a clue concerning where to look for work and the fact that I was 43 years old. While I mulled over these thoughts and prayers we went to pick up Daddy so he could spend some time with us. He was still mourning Miss Lillie's death and I thought it would do him good to get away.

Shortly after lunch one day the phone rang. It was Jane. She asked me if I would be interested in a bookkeeping job at the local school where she taught. I quickly replied that I surely would because I needed to help the kids with their school expenses. The only way I had of making any money was to substitute for the teachers now and then. That was hard work and very little pay. She told me that the school principal/teacher said for me to come up for an interview after school that day. I learned later that Jane came through the office to make copies on the old duplicator when the principal asked her if she knew of anyone who would be interested in the job. Things were happening fast and I thought if I get this job God is really in the business of answering prayers fast. I was hired that afternoon and came home excited. Of course, Johnny did not speak of my part-time job very highly. He referred to it as my penny-ante job. I took a thick book with instructions about preparing the lunch report and studied it diligently. The office personnel at the school board congratulated me for getting all the paper work done correctly that was sent to the state and for getting the payroll in on time. It boosted my morale to know that I could succeed at work and I did indeed enjoy being around the students and teachers without having the responsibility of keeping them in line while trying to get their lessons across. The next year the supervisor asked me to work at two other small schools and to make Elsanor my base school. I would be a full time employee. She also asked the superintendent for mileage for my travel expenses to the other schools. I liked the challenge of balancing the long reports.

As time passed I received raises and after the first year the Board of Education took retirement out of my check. Over the years I was able to save money in the credit union to purchase things for the house such as two oriental rugs, new kitchen appliances and den furniture. Johnny retired from NAS in 1985 so if he needed me to drive to load hay in the evenings I was available or if there were vegetables to pick and can with his help I could get through before bedtime. Late one October evening I was driving the tractor while he loaded hay in the bright moonlight. He called for me to "Whoa" when I thought he said, "Go" and I ran over his foot. Luckily he was wearing his boots with steel toes.

I especially liked helping the students at Elsanor Elementary. If I became aware that a child needed glasses that his family could not afford, I looked for organizations to pay for them. There were times when I picked splinters from hands, doctored sores and burns and put band-aids on scraped knees. I even carried Epson salt to school so a boy could soak his infected toe until I could get in touch with the school nurse to take him to the doctor. It was my privilege to sit beside children who were injured in P.E. and wipe tears from their eyes until their mother arrived. I was able to help sixth grade teacher, Mrs. Kathy Barnhill and the parents decorate for sixth grade graduation and secure speakers. Although my job was not considered very important I took nothing for granted when the principal was over two schools and I was the only one in the office at Elsanor for one half day. I took my job seriously and tried to keep things running smoothly when he was not there.

The red brick school where my children received their elementary education and where I substituted and later started working burned to the ground on a cold night in November of 1985. When someone called us at four in the morning and told us the school was on fire, I could hardly believe it. My job there drastically changed. The office where I worked was gone. The files, reports, checkbooks and all sorts of forms were burned. The fire marshal said it was arson. When those guilty were found it turned out to be two former students. A few things they had stolen were found in their car. They were put in jail and many changes had to be made in order to keep the school in session. My office was in a small room in the first one-room school that had been placed on the grounds for a teacherage and later used as a Kindergarten room. Portable buildings were moved in for the teachers and students. It took months for me to get the reports up-to-date but I received a good audit that year. After the new school was constructed I had a nice office with red cabinets, an intercom system and new furniture. I cried when the old school burned but the new school was a better facility.

I found the job very rewarding and looked forward to helping the principals, students and parents. When I retired in 1993 because of health issues I had worked for three different principals at Elsanor School, Mr. Ronnie Green, Mr. Ed Comer and Mr. Joel Erlandson. I also became friends with Swift School's Principal Marie Carver, whom I worked with for nine years. I also worked for Principal Arabella Rachel at Swift School. Principal Byron Lee retired after my first year at Bell Fountain School and I then enjoyed working with Principal Patricia Peterson. We also became very good friends. The teachers and students at Elsanor Elementary sent me off with bang. The PTA presented me with a bird bath, a plant and a plaque. The teachers and staff hosted a retirement luncheon for me at Ivy's Fine Dining after school was out. I was able to purchase new drapes and a nice tablecloth and napkins for the dining room with the large gift certificate they gave me to Gayfer's Department Store. I was still using the same drapes I bought when we moved into the house over 25 years ago. I received the thrill of my life when I was honored at the sixth grade graduation a few days before my retirement. I had no idea that they had contacted my daughter to slip in and sing "Wind Beneath my Wings." One of the students read a poem they wrote for me and had framed. I have always thanked God for my small retirement check and the productive years of my life when I could work, still keep a clean house, do my children's laundry and ironing and cook them good meals when they came home from college. You might say I had a dream job. The student's helped me in various ways and the teachers, staff and parents became my friends. Mothers volunteered to help in other ways on busy days. And the most important thing was that the principals trusted me. I believed in strictly going by the rules. When I worked at the school in my community for three days out of the week I was only a mile away from home and could be at work in five minutes.

42
To Farm or Not to Farm

Grandchildren playing on a load of hay their Grandpa baled
and Sean riding the tractor with him.

One summer around 1970 we planted corn and soybeans as usual. Mr. Clark at Robertsdale Feed Store always obliged us by letting us charge the fertilizer and seed at his store. We prayed for a good year because we still needed furniture for the new house and we wanted to save what we could for Barry's college expenses when he enrolled in college in 1972. I could see the corn growing as I gazed out my bedroom window each morning as I made my bed. Things seemed to be going smooth until suddenly the weather got hot and very dry. We did not receive rain on the crops when we needed it. I would stand on the front porch and look for one little rain cloud and pray for rain. Then one evening Barry came home limping from his karate lessons. He had been kicked on his shin the week before and then received another blow to the same sore spot that night. By morning his leg was very swollen and painful so I took him to the doctor to get it checked out. The diagnosis was a blood clot in his leg. The doctor immediately admitted him to the hospital and said that he must stay in bed at all times. When he said that Barry could not get out of bed I became very concerned. I knew that blood clots could move to the heart or lungs. I began praying that he would be alright. In fact, I lifted up a prayer to God promising Him that if He would just help my son to get well, He could take the corn crop.

After several days in the hospital Barry did get to come home but still had to stay off his leg as much as possible. I was so relieved. However, we did not get any rain until it was too late. The corn burned up in the field. I realized that I had rather my son be healthy and alive than have the corn to sell. So I always knew God answered my prayer for my good. The next year we planted soybeans in that same field. We did get some rain on the soybeans, but we discovered that nematodes had attacked the roots of the plants and we did not have a good yield. Other farmers in the county were enduring the same hardships. The drought had hit them hard several years in a row and had spread throughout the South. We were not making enough money to pay the seed, fertilizer, combining and spraying bills. We pondered what we should do. Johnny got in touch with the soil conservation agent and asked him to pay us a visit. He had been out to our farm before in years past when we received too much rain and the top soil in the fields washed away leaving deep ditches. Since the land was sandy and the soil very erodible the conservationist advised Johnny to begin planting Bahia grass for pasture and buy a few head of cattle at the time to eat the grass. He also advised that terraces be built to help with erosion. Johnny had lived his dream of being a row-crop farmer and God had blessed his endeavors. Now God was telling him it was time for him to take another route and be a herdsman of cattle. He had given him the land to farm and now He had been showing him little by little that he must lay aside the farm equipment and not work so hard. There would still be hay to be baled in order to have feed for the cattle but since he had injured his knee while in the Air Force and later his elbow as a civil service worker and had gone through so many surgeries during his lifetime it was time that he took life a little easier. Johnny had made the right decision, but I doubted he would ever stop being the workaholic I knew him to be.

43
The Truck that Floated on Water

Johnny drove his Datsun truck for years after it rolled into the pond with hay on it.

After Johnny retired from his job at NAS he kept busy taking care of the cattle and doing odd jobs around the farm. He had taken Real Estate classes from Mr. Perdue in Gulf Shores and they had become friends. He first received his real estate license and worked at Perdue Realty for awhile until he passed his brokers test and got a license so he could open an office on the farm. We had decided to sell some of our farm land since he had cut back on farming after retirement. It seems to me that he wanted to enter other facets of business and was thoroughly enjoying meeting other people. He became very active in politics and even decided to run for county commission one year. We attended all the rallies and he made his speeches but the incumbent went back in office. I did not let him know that I was praying that he would seek other avenues of interest because there was so much confusion among the politicians that year and it would have been a busy, stressful job.

One afternoon he went down to the pasture to feed the cattle with 15 bales of hay on the back of the Datsun pick-up truck. At the time he was recovering from surgery on his knee that he injured when he fell from the top of a load of hay. His knee cap slipped off when he fell and tore the tendons and ligaments. We made a flying trip by car to Columbus, Georgia to the famous Houston Clinic where he had painful knee surgery. He was sporting a cast on his leg and walked with crutches. I usually climbed on the back of the truck at feeding time and threw the hay to the cows but Johnny told me he could manage that evening.

As soon as the cows saw the little blue farm truck coming they started running as fast as they could to meet their master who supplied their supper. He could not drive in the pasture without the cows bombarding him. They always thought it was feeding time anytime he drove to the ponds. Johnny got out of the truck and began throwing two bales of hay for the hungry cows to start munching on. They wanted it all at once and began to pull at the remaining 13 bales. Suddenly without warning the truck started rolling down the hill. Johnny stood there helpless because he could not run to catch the truck since he was on crutches. The truck picked up speed as it rolled on down the hill breaking a four strand barbed-wire fence. It continued picking up speed as it rolled until it went into the fish pond with 13 bales of hay still on the back. The cattle were unconcerned as they fought over the two bales of hay as Johnny stared in amazement as the truck began floating across the pond. It kept floating until it struck the side of the dam where it sank. The stack of hay floated off the truck and held together. Johnny stood on the dam in disbelief as he gazed at the CB antenna on the truck protruding out of the pond water. It remained the only indication there was a sunken truck beneath the water.

Johnny realized that he must do something quickly so with crutches under his arms he began his slow trek up the hill to the house which stood a quarter of a mile away. At least he had taken them out when he began feeding. When he reached home he called his sister, Ruth and brother-in-law, Otto to bring their truck and tractor to pull the truck out of the water. They loaded Johnny's Jon-boat and carried it down to the pond. Otto and Johnny climbed in the boat and Otto went into the pond and stood in the back of the truck. He ducked his head under the water to hook a chain to the back truck bumper. Once out of the water Otto climbed on the tractor and pulled the truck up to the dam, but was unable to pull it out because his tractor was spinning and rearing up. He shouted for Johnny to open the truck doors to let the water out to make the truck lighter. The force of the water almost knocked Johnny down but it worked. The little Datsun then weighed less and the tractor gradually began pulling the water soaked vehicle over the dam of the pond and on up to the house.

As for the 13 bales of hay they continued floating around the pond for days. When they got the truck home they drained the diesel fuel and oil from the motor and changed the fuel filters several times. They also pulled the fuel injectors from the engine and rotated the engine with the starter in order to blow all of the water out of the cylinders. On the second day the truck sputtered and spit a bit and then turned the motor over and cranked much to Johnny's surprise. He drove it to town for a service station attendant to change the oil in the rear axle. I was really astounded because I thought we would have to junk the truck.

After that tune-up he drove the truck for ten more years until he sold it. When Johnny witnessed his little diesel truck roll into his pond he never dreamed it would ever run again, but miracles still happen even when we think the situation is impossible. He still talks about his little truck that could float on water.

44
Empty Nest Syndrome

Jeanette with Dusty after their afternoon walk

The house was quiet and still on this chilly night of January, 1981. John and I sat in our recliners by the fireside with only the sound of the crackling fire and the voice of the news anchorman penetrating the den. Occasionally I took my eyes off the afghan I was crocheting and quit counting the clusters of singles, doubles and trebles. My mind kept wandering to the unforeseeable future as I asked myself the question concerning what lay in store for the three children who had brought such happiness, fulfillment and even confrontational discussions into our lives. It was clear I was suffering from "Empty Nest Syndrome."

During the year of 1980, all three of our offspring made major decisions to search for a life of their own. Our second son, Doyle, with his outgoing personality and love of sports and cravings for his freedom from farm life to city life had asked to move to an apartment near the college he was attending in Mobile, Alabama. Shortly before this time while working a summer job at Gulf Shores he had met a lovely young girl from Mobile and after graduation from Faulkner State Jr. College had transferred to the University of South Alabama. On a beautiful spring day on May 10, 1980, they were married in an afternoon ceremony at Springhill Baptist Church. They moved into a small townhouse and set up housekeeping.

We were happy for Twila that she had a chance to start college on a scholarship at Troy State, but all too soon it was time for me to help pack her necessities in her little red Ford Mustang. I would make the trip with her to help get her settled in a campus dorm with her best friend, Vickie Comer, with whom she graduated. Vickie's mother, Loyce, and I felt they would be secure when we bade them good bye at TSU and headed home, but my, how I would miss my last born.

Barry, our oldest son, was considered a home-boy, who was of tremendous help to his Dad on the 150 acres he farmed while also holding down a full time job as an Aircraft Mechanic at Pensacola Naval Air Station. Barry liked staying at home and eating my cooking and we in turn enjoyed having him with us. In his spare time he went hunting and fishing. After five years of college and a Master's degree to show for his perseverance, he had landed a job as a teacher in Mobile County. He was proud of the new truck he was able to purchase. Barry had been dating Charlene Peckham, whom he met at our church. They were married just before Christmas on a freezing night on December 20, 1980. They rented a small apartment in Mobile, Alabama, where they would both teach school.

After returning my thoughts to the present, I rose from my chair and walked through the rooms of this now vacant, orderly house. I observed the neatness of what we referred to as the kid's bathroom. It looked strange without the hair rollers, blow dryers and wet towels hanging lopsided on racks. No make up, razors, toothbrushes or open toothpaste tubes cluttered the counters.

In the boy's bedroom I found two empty undisturbed oak beds. The usual rumpled matching blue bedspreads showed no signs of wrinkles. Gone were the shoes, socks, and assorted clothing strewn all over the room. No radios and books were crammed on their desk. Only a few favorite model airplanes, miniature cars and other small items on the shelves left behind would remind me that this had been the sleeping quarters of my two sons who had such different interests. My daughter's room no longer looked like a storage room for a museum or a zoo. The stuffed animals collected over her lifetime that would not fit in her dorm lay silently in place on the mint green comforter of her neatly made bed. Everything was in its place awaiting her return some convenient weekend.

I mused, could I ever learn to cook only a few biscuits, two pork chops and enough rice and gravy for two? I possibly might manage reducing the other food, but not a small pan of corn bread. Never! Twila's faithful dog, Dusty, missed her so. He would meet me at the back door wagging his tail when I returned from my job in the afternoon. I knew he was thinking, "Can we take a walk?" He especially missed his afternoon run behind Twila on her horse, Shatata. They often rode the wooded trails and fields of our farm freely. I needed the exercise so off we would go with Dusty sniffing the fencerows to be sure they were free of snakes. I was always engrossed in observing the beauty of the lush green pastures with grazing cattle. I thought of the beautiful white wild roses that would cascade from the swamp trees near the ponds as we walked in springtime. On this day just to hear the caw of the crow in the late afternoon was a welcome sound. It seemed good to have a time of quiet meditation, and thankfulness to God for his abundant blessings upon my family after a busy day at work.

My children had been granted an opportunity of a college education that their father and I never dreamed of achieving because of hard times, lack of funds and responsibilities. Our two boys were settling down with careers and our daughter beginning a new learning adventure.

I stayed busy at my job at three small schools, with volunteer work, serving the Lord in my church and housekeeping, but it seemed that all at once I was not needed so much anymore. I knew I would somehow find a way to move on, except the changes for the better and look forward to the future. I would relish a time when they would bring sweet grandchildren to this farm for me to love and rock. Maybe I would even have more time to read books to my grandchildren or play with them and their toys on the floor than I did with my children. I surmised I would anticipate each visit.

So for now I must settle for cooking special dishes for Twila's new found college friends and welcome them into this house. I would await the visits of my newly wed sons and daughters-in-law. Once again I would hear the sound of voices, stereos, showers running and blow dryers humming. Even wet towels on the floor would not bother me. Until then I would be at peace knowing I did my best to love, teach and nurture my precious gifts from God.

45
The Joys Grandchildren Bring

Grandma poses with Christina and Whitney

Granddaughters dance to Jingle Bells

Later Heather, Joshua, & Hannah joined Tina & Whit

Sean was the Sixth Grandchild.

Celebrating Easter with the Grands.

Christmas, 1996 we wore Noah's Ark T-shirts.

I looked forward to the day when I would become a grandmother. I did not ask my daughters-in-law, "When?" I knew that they needed to work and help with household expenses for a few years, but I was thrilled the day Barry and Charlene came over and excitedly told us they were expecting a baby. As a "grandmother to be," I hurried off to Wal-Mart to purchase crochet thread to start making a baby blanket. I had no idea if the baby would be a boy or girl so I chose a thread color that either sex could use. Never mind that I had several months to finish the blanket, it was just important that I got it finished before there was a baby shower.

It was a Friday night October 14, 1983, when I got the call from Barry who lived in Mobile telling me that he was taking Charlene to the hospital. As much as I had looked forward to the baby's arrival, it was a little hectic for me to drop everything and take off quickly, but I did. Twila, and two new friends, Julie and Sherry, had just arrived from Troy State for the weekend.

Fortunately, we had just finished what they called a good home cooked meal and were washing dishes when the call came. We got the kitchen cleaned in a flash and John, and I, took off for Mobile. I did not worry about hosting Twila's company because they planned to take in the Shrimp Festival in Gulf Shores on Saturday and there were plenty of leftovers in the refrigerator. I really wanted to be there so I could be among the first to view my grandchild so Johnny and I left in a hurry. It did not concern me whether the baby was a boy or a girl. I had only prayed that he or she would be healthy. We settled down in the waiting room of the hospital on chairs that were much too firm and began our long vigil with Charlene's mother, Loretta. Unfortunately, her dad and brother had left earlier that day for Tuscaloosa to attend an Alabama football game the next day. This baby would be their second grandchild.

Every so often, Barry would put his head in the door of the waiting room and give us an update. He said it may be a long night and so it was. Loretta was tired from a busy day of housecleaning and I had worked hard trying to get everything caught up at the schools in case I missed a few days work so we tried to rest after a long night of anticipation. I must have dozed off sometime before morning because I sat up straight as I realized the sun was streaming through the windows of the waiting room. It had been a night of apprehension and concern and now they were telling us that Charlene's doctor was going to his office to see some patients. When we heard this news we all became upset because it was Saturday and the doctor's office should be closed? We took turns going to the cafeteria to get a bite of breakfast, then hurried back to wait again on the hard chairs that had our bones aching. Needless to say we were worried.

Finally about mid afternoon on Saturday a nurse appeared and announced we had a granddaughter. I jumped up to run find the correct room number, but Johnny and Loretta outran me. Drat it! I was disappointed that I would not be the first to gaze upon the face of the new miracle of life God had so graciously given to our family. But when I saw our baby I thought she was the most beautiful baby I had ever laid eyes on. It did not matter that her head was a little lopsided and her face somewhat red and swollen. Her thick dark hair and bright blue eyes told me she was fine. I said a prayer of thankfulness that she was finally in our world. When I declared that our little darling was the most beautiful baby in the world I knew all grandparents thought the same thing about their grandchildren and I realized I was prejudiced. We took turns holding baby Christina Leigh Ryan. Yes, indeed, this baby would be dearly loved and cherished.

A few weeks later, I awoke one Saturday morning to the sweet cooing of little Christina as she lay in the other bedroom between her parents who had brought her for her first visit. I had already taken the twin bed down and put up a baby bed in the boy's former bedroom. I got out of bed and hurried with breakfast because I could not wait to cuddle and rock my new granddaughter. It did not matter whether or not the breakfast dishes got washed; I was determined to spend as much time with Christina as I could. She was already gaining weight and changing.

When Christina was a little older, I had the privilege of babysitting her at times. As soon as she began to talk, her first words when she arrived at Grandpa's and Grandma's were: "Outside" and "Birds." Her grandpa had taken her out to show her his many different colored pigeons and had repeated the word "Bird" over and over again to her. The next time she visited she had not forgotten. When she was a little older I got out a box of old toys that my children had played with many years ago and the two of us sat on the den rug and lined up all of the animals, trucks, cars and other toys around us and I sang out "I Love A Parade" as we beat on a little drum. I decided Tina was bringing me a lot of sunshine, so one weekend I kept singing, "You Are My Sunshine," to her but she seemed unconcerned or so I thought. The next week her mother wanted to know where she learned the song because she had been singing it to them after they went home.

After that, every time Christina was left in my care, while I was cooking dinner, she played with the toys and began to make up her own songs. I was amazed that at three years of age she could carry a tune and sometime the verses even rhymed. One cold winter weekend Charlene accompanied Barry on a trip to our hunting camp in central Alabama. I was excited to have my granddaughter stay all weekend, but also a little apprehensive because her mother informed me before they left that Christina had a bit of a cold. I was to give her a half teaspoon of her medicine if her sniffles worsened. That first night Christina and I cuddled up in a soft bed with all of Twila's Dr. Seuss books I could find. I read and read as she took in every word. If I tried to skip a line she noticed. If I stopped reading, she finished the page because her mother had read her the same books. I became drowsy a long time before she did so she shook me to wake me up and finish the story. The next day because she was sniffling a little, I felt I needed to give her some of her medicine before I went to the grocery store. As soon as I started strapping her in the grocery buggy, she fell over asleep. I had given the medicine in a measuring spoon as I had been instructed but; she slept all afternoon. I never told her parents that the medicine over-dosed their baby.

Almost two weeks after Christina's second birthday, our second granddaughter, Whitney Tucker Ryan, was born in Mobile on October 28, 1985. It was not very long before her arrival. Of course, she too, was beautiful and a precious little bundle of joy. We began to look forward to Easter and Christmas because suddenly the holidays became so much more fun with two little girls to fuss over. One Christmas we purchased both of them rocky horses and they laughed and rocked until bedtime. Whitney had come into the world dancing. We attended a Gospel singing one Saturday night when we were babysitting her. She was only 16 months old but she got out of my lap, stood on the floor and began clapping her hands and dancing to the music. The people in the audience took their eyes off the stage and began watching her. I knew then that she had a special kind of rhythm. The Christmas when Christina was four and Whitney was two years old, I got my old Gene Autry and Bing Crosby 78 RPM records and played them in the living room. The girls were playing by the Christmas tree in the living room. They did not see us watching from the kitchen as they began to dance to "Jingle Bell Rock." Their Aunt Twila videoed them as they danced and we watched the tape on Christmas Eve for years, much to their displeasure.

Since our granddaughters were both born in October, we celebrated their third and fifth birthdays at our house on a Saturday. We tied balloons to the big oak tree and set everything up in the yard. As the girls stood on chairs behind the table with the birthday cake and gifts, Christina reached over and gave Whitney a big hug and kiss. Of course, it was spontaneous, but we happened to get a snapshot of that moment in time.

Whitney spent the week after Christmas with us for several years.

She wanted Christina to join us so they could play together. The three of us spent many happy hours playing imaginary or made-up games on the front porch. The girls would tumble through my closets and drag out old clothes, shoes, flowers for their hair and costume jewelry to dress up like brides. As they grew older they wrote their own plays. When they had perfected and practiced them they would fetch me from the kitchen to be their audience while they performed. Whitney was usually some poor outcast that, Tina, the rich lady rescued and helped survive.

They both were very bright but had different personalities. Whitney thrived on performing and dancing, while Tina was more reserved and had rather cuddle up with a good book. They were always learning. We baked cookies and played board games together. I decided since these two were so much fun, I could stand being grandmother to a few more bundles of joy.

46

The Patter of Other Little Feet

Joshua, Hannah and Heather
at play

Sean with Grandma holding
baby Noah

I was busy catching up on my reports at Elsanor Elementary School one May morning when I got the call from my son, Barry informing me that he was taking Charlene to the hospital for the birth of their second child. It appeared that Hannah was going to be born on May 26, 1988. That was Johnny's mother's birthday. I hurried to call a substitute to work for me and to inform the principal. Then I excitedly got in touch with Johnny to let him know him I was on my way home so he could get dressed to go to the hospital. We did not have to wait long after we got to Thomas Hospital before our third granddaughter was born. Her parents named her, Hannah Marie. Charlene's parents, Pat and Loretta Peckham were there, too so we took turns gearing up with the mask and gowns so we could see Charlene and hold the baby. When it came my time, I took the little newborn baby girl in my arms and looked into her big blue eyes. She too, like the others was beautiful with black hair covering her head. I wondered to myself what God had in store for her as she grew. I had big dreams for my three granddaughters and any grandsons I might have in the future.

Our first grandson, Joshua Christopher Bilon arrived just before Christmas on December 12, 1988 on the same date of my Daddy's birthday. Twila had been visiting us that Sunday and left at dark to go home. It was not long before we found out they were headed to the hospital. As Twila's mother, I was worried but she came through like a trooper. We gazed through the nursery window at a round faced chubby little bald headed boy. Since he was our first grandson, we were excited about his birth and could not wait to hold him. I took a week's leave from work and went to stay with them so I could help take care of Joshua and also do some cleaning and cooking. I had many chances to rock him in the new white wicker rocker we gave them for Christmas. Twila recovered in time for them to bring Joshua to spend Christmas Eve with us. I volunteered to babysit as much as possible because it was so much fun watching them grow. Joshua was a happy little boy and since he went in high gear as he scooted around so fast in his walker he had several minor accidents with bumps and bruises. It seemed he never crawled much before he started running everywhere he went. We were keeping him one day when he came running down the hall so fast that he stumbled and hit the corner of the brick fireplace making a deep gash on his forehead. He was tough though and never cried much when he had an accident. Since Johnny's mother had passed away in 1984 and my daddy died in 1986, I felt as if the Lord had taken and that He was now giving back to our family by giving us grandchildren on their birthdays.

A year after Hannah's birth, the following May 25, 1989, we were on standby again in order to babysit Christina and Hannah when their little baby sister arrived. I hurried over to get Hannah just as they left for the hospital in order to pick up Christina at one of the teacher's homes in Belforest. The teacher had brought her from Spanish Fort School where Barry taught third grade and Christina attended school. I brought the girls to my house where I would keep them in the den after I fed them because Twila and some friends had planned a Lingerie shower for her close friend, Kathy

Hedden. We did not interfere with the shower since Twila had set it all up in the living room. Before the girls left the shower I found out that we had another little granddaughter. They named her Heather Lynn. The granddaughters now numbered four to one grandson, so Grandpa Ryan was still hoping for a couple more grandsons. I spent the weekend with Barry and Charlene. On Friday and Saturday Barry and I did the laundry and cleaned the house to make ready for Charlene and the new baby's homecoming. Hannah missed her mother so she clung to me and followed me wherever I went. I was pretty busy but would take time to comfort her and hold her when I could because she was only a year old and did not understand why her mother had abandoned her. On Sunday I cooked a good dinner since we had been eating quick meals. Later their friends came to see the new baby and made plans to bring food the next week.

On November 3, 1992 I was busy at work that Tuesday when I picked up the phone on the first ring. Barry was on the line calling for me to come over to take care of the other children. He said he needed to hurry and get Charlene to the hospital. Their fourth child was ready to make his appearance. Barry had called earlier to tell me to be on standby because they had made one false alarm trip to Thomas Hospital that morning. The doctor advised Charlene to go home and rest until later when it was time to return. Since it was the first Tuesday of November Charlene and Barry stopped by the town hall in Silverhill to vote. Finally about 3:00 pm Barry called me to hurry over because they had almost waited to long to leave. He got her in the front seat of the van and sped off. I prayed they would make it to the hospital in time. Before I could prepare the girls a light supper they called me. Barry was now the proud Daddy of a son. His three little girls seemed so excited. The doctor had advised them that the baby would be a big baby and he certainly was. Sean Barrett Ryan weighed in at 10 pounds, 6 ounces. The next afternoon I carried all three of the girls to Thomas Hospital to meet their little brother. Christina and Hannah took turns holding Sean, but Heather would have no part of it. She stayed in her Daddy's arms with a slight frown on her face not understanding why her mother had suddenly gone to bed and things had changed so quickly. I suppose she was somewhat jealous that someone so small could take her place so quickly and turn her world upside down. In time she became adjusted to having a brother to love on and play with.

John Noah arrived on September 7, 1996. It had been a difficult time for Charlene. Her doctor had ordered her to bed. Barry would get up early and make breakfast for the girls and then they would all hurry to Spanish Fort Elementary School. He would either bring Sean to my house or I would leave early enough to get to their house before Sean woke. I helped out as much as I could, so between all of us we managed until Noah's birth. Noah was a big baby, too since he also weighed over 10 pounds. As babies, the brothers favored so much. Now I can hardly tell one from the other when I look at their baby pictures, but there is not much resemblance since they have grown. Grandpa Ryan was ecstatic when Barry and Charlene named the baby John Noah. That made four generations of Johns in the Ryan family. Johnny's daddy was John William Ryan, Sr., Johnny was John William Ryan, Jr. and Barry was John Barry Ryan with John Noah the fourth generation. Sean is very mechanically inclined and stays busy with his projects while Noah enjoys fishing, hunting and playing ball. Sean enrolled at Faulkner Community College this year and Noah enrolled in the eighth grade at Central Baldwin Middle School. It seems only yesterday they were Grandma's little babies. Now that the girls are grown and married I now wait to see which one will make me a great-grandmother. I know I have to be patient, but I am ready.

47
Highlights from Christmas Letters 1989 to 2011

Christmas is Coming

Christmas is coming! We feel it in the air,
Everyone's shopping and wrapping presents with care,
They're putting up Christmas trees with ornaments shiny and bright,
And hanging lights on porches and in towns to shine in the night.

The kitchens all have a special aroma of cookies, cakes and pies,
Gifts under the trees make the kids want to peek and spy.
The grandchildren seem extra helpful, cheerful and good.
If it wasn't for that long wish list, I wonder if they would.

I'm sitting here in my chair by the cozy warm fire
Not wanting to face the pushing and shoving out there
I just want to enjoy the season until it is over and past
Because the message of the Christ Child is all that will last.

December, 1989: Johnny is Recovering after a Fall and Surgery

This cold, wet, December day finds us sitting in a hotel in Columbus, Georgia. Johnny is back here for a follow-up visit after his knee surgery. He fell off a trailer load of hay and dislocated his knee as they were loading the last few bales on October 23rd. He had filled two barns with hay and this was to be his last load. He wanted to come to the famous Houston Clinic for surgery since all the ligaments and tendons in his knee were torn loose. Thankfully, he had finished planting the winter pasture before the accident. I missed a week's work so I had to catch up before Christmas. I had been sick with a bad sinus infection when we left for Georgia that left me with a bad cough. I drove us home with a splitting headache.

Little Joshua celebrated his first birthday last Sunday with his mom preparing a brunch for family members. His birthday on December 12 is a memorable time for me. Barry and Charlene's newest addition to the family, Heather Lynn Ryan, was born last May 25 just one day before her sister, Hannah's first birthday on May 26. Barry finally landed a teaching job in Baldwin County after teaching in Mobile for 10 years. Doyle's job at a bank keeps him very busy but he still found time to get an eight point deer when the season started. We are looking forward to seeing Whitney along with all the other grandchildren at Christmas.

We have received many blessings this year! Love, Grandma and Grandpa Ryan

Christmas: 1990 Celebrating the Jubilee

God has blessed us. Johnny is finally walking without a cane after last October's accident. I have been very busy at work but I enjoy my job. Enrollment at our school is increasing since this area is really growing. I spend my free time writing the history of my church which I thoroughly enjoy doing. Bethel will celebrate the 50 year "Jubilee" in 1991. The grandchildren are growing and are so much fun. The good news is Whitney started Kindergarten last fall, but the bad news was that Christina recently broke her arm while playing on Johnny's exercise equipment. We hate to see them hurt. For entertainment this Christmas Twila and Christina will be playing their keyboards while we sing Christmas carols before we have our family devotion.

Remember the reason for the season, Love, Jeanette and Johnny

December, 1992 Johnny Dabbles in Politics and Real Estate,

Our family is rejoicing in the birth of another grandson. Sean Barrett Ryan born on November 3, 1992. Grandpa hurried to the hospital when he heard the news thinking about his first Ryan grandson to carry on the name. Grandma rushed to pick up the girls to keep while Charlene was in the hospital. Johnny ran for County Commissioner in the May Primary, but did not get enough votes to beat the incumbent. He still keeps up with county politics and runs his real estate office. Johnny and Barry are surveying a small sub-division to sell. We had home-grown Christmas trees this year from the farm and have planted almost 40 acres of pine trees on our land. We also sold some of the cows. Merry Christmas, Jeanette & John

1993: Jeanette Retires from her Job

Johnny is enjoying racing his 200 plus homing pigeons with a Pensacola pigeon racing club along with his deer hunting. He had to have his fifth knee surgery in Birmingham in August so he is still limping as he takes care of his cattle, farm chores and real estate business. He is now a real estate broker and works from his office at home. Since I last wrote you I have retired from my job as school secretary in July due to health issues. Retirement was not in my plans this year but I prayed and I know God helped me make the right decision. I miss the students, faculty and parents. After seeing several doctors, a rheumatologist finally diagnosed my condition as Fibromyalgia. I am presently in therapy and hope to keep active in my community, church and by spending time with the grandchildren.

Joy, Peace, Blessings, Jeanette and Johnny

December, 1994: Snow in February in Lower Alabama,

This year my hobby has been compiling scrapbooks. I made one with pictures and notes of Mama's family, the Shumocks' and one of Daddy's family, the Dyess clan. It has been a busy year. In January, I participated in Elsanor School's Heritage Day program by telling the school's history. Since retirement I had a chance to update the history of Elsanor School that a friend started. The dates ranged from the school's beginning in 1913 to the present. February - Awoke to a brilliant wonderland of snow. The farm looked like a picture of the north since snow is rare in Lower Alabama. March – Spent a delightful day at Twila's church where they honored her for her Christian work. I presented her with a scrapbook I made. April – The Ryan and Peckham families joined together for a wonderful Easter dinner at Barry's and Charlene's. May – Had a delicious Mother's Day supper at Twila and Chris' new home near Silverhill. Johnny was feeling badly from loading hay in the hot sun. He had to be admitted to the hospital the next day because he was suffering from dehydration. June – I had a lovely surprise on Sunday, June 7, 1994. It started with a 60th birthday dinner at Barry's and Charlene's. Following lunch we gathered at Twila and Chris' home. As I entered the door there were 60 friends and relatives waiting inside to surprise me and help celebrate my birthday. They had prepared wonderful refreshments and Twila sang and played a song she wrote for me. July – We attended the Ryan Reunion at Ryan's Crossroads in north Alabama. Johnny's nephew, Lee Ryan, flew down from California to join us. We picked up Athel and Alene Ryan from Birmingham, and traveled together. August – A fine time spent with Dyess relatives as I hosted a dinner at my house for around 30 relatives. September – My brother, Ernest Dyess' book titled, *"God if you're real, let the cow be in the pen when I get home"* was published. I pray that people will come to know the Lord when they read it. October – Aunt Alma and her daughter, Sharon, gave Uncle Willis Dyess a birthday party that was well attended. November – Our kids and grandkids spent Thanksgiving here with us on the farm. It was a beautiful, balmy day. December –the WMU ladies met at my home for the Week of Prayer for Foreign Missions meeting and later Johnny's pigeon club members came for a Christmas supper and party.

That's all folks. Come to see us. Love, Jeanette and John

December: 1995 My Most Memorable Christmas

My most memorable Christmas I suppose was the first Christmas in our new house which we built in 1966-67. We had no living room furniture but we had bright, shiny new hardwood floors to put our Christmas tree on. The church gave us a housewarming on a cold, crisp day in December. Johnny had planted winter rye on the front lawn where the soybeans grew. We were the only neighbors with a green lawn that freezing December day. Ruth helped me decorate the mantels and doors with greenery. I was happy that I had finished making drapes for all the windows except the beige living room drapes we purchased. We received many beautiful gifts for our home that were put to use. Celebrating Christmas Eve with our kids, my daddy and Johnny's mother that year was an evening I will never forget.

Happy Holidays, the Ryans

Christmas-1996: Twila Writes and Records Songs

My, how the days of 1996 have flown away never to return. Thankfully, I am recovering from unexpected gall bladder surgery. I was happy to leave the hospital in time to make it to Twila's for Thanksgiving dinner. Johnny had finished baling and storing a barn full of hay when unfortunately lightning struck and killed 20 of his herd where they gathered under a tree. Last summer Twila sang and recorded 10 songs that she had written in Nashville. Joshua sang one of the songs on the tape. She has ministered by singing the songs in churches, schools, luncheons and community events. Barry and Charlene bought property and built a home in Elsanor about 10 miles from us. My cousin, Nelda Dyess Rezner and her husband, Rudy hosted a "Bull Springs Reunion" in November for all the neighbors who lived in the Bull Springs community when we were growing up. We had such an enjoyable time telling old tales and reminiscing. Whitney's dance performance team won many first place positions as they danced at Disney World.

1997: Christmas on the Farm

Christmas on our farm is such a peaceful warm tradition
As the family gathers here to celebrate Jesus birth and mission,
Every Christmas Eve Grandma cooks the annual turkey dinner
While waiting for the grandchildren bundled in their winter splendor.

The gifts are piled high around the blinking Christmas tree.
Hannah, Heather, Joshua and Sean are filled with excitement and glee,
While Christina and Whitney contemplate, "What's in this box for me?"
They can hardly wait until we eat, so they can peek and see.

Since last year in September, another little miracle has arrived.
He has sparkling blue eyes and the sweetest great big smile.
John Noah is the fourth generation of John Ryan's to carry on the name.
His dad and grandpa are very proud, but he is loved by all the same.

We sit by the fire, sing Christmas carols and read Luke's story,
Then we thank God for sending his son with all his divine glory,
We will pass out all the presents we had so much fun selecting,
We hope everyone is pleased and received what they expected.

We watch squirrels from the windows as they look for acorns way up high,
A flock of homing pigeons are circling and gliding up in the clear blue sky,
While the cows are munching their daily portion of hay brought from the barn
All our celebration and anticipation gives them no cause for alarm.

It will be so much fun celebrating Christmas with a Noah's Ark theme this year,"
We will all wear shirts signifying how God saved the animals and told us not to fear,
For He would never again destroy the earth with water, but would send a rainbow
And best of all a Savior that would be born in Bethlehem on a night so long ago.
God Bless, Jeanette and John

1999: Approaching the Millennium

Only a few more days remain in 1999. As we approach the millennium, The Year of our Lord, 2000, I look back in time to recall when I was a child how very far away that seemed. As I enter the new millennium I want to thank God for the many blessings, both physically and spiritually he has bestowed on one such as I. We stay busy trying to keep up this farm. John's menagerie of animals consist of: 1 gawking guinea who serves as a watch dog, 2 German white chickens that lay green eggs, 3 beautiful strutting peacocks, 8 Quacking Mallard ducks, 10 Cooing white doves, 30 head of lowing cattle, and several hundred gorgeous homing pigeons. Noah, our youngest grandson, spent the day with us last week. He was playing in the leaves Grandpa was raking and helping Grandma pick-up pecans when suddenly he took his little bucket of pecans and poured them over the pasture fence. I asked him why he did that. He replied, "I feed cows." He had seen his grandpa throw hay over the fence to the cows so he decided to help feed them, too. Johnny has stocked up on canned goods and toilet paper in case something spectacular happens. Take care and enjoy the New Year. From the two of us who make our home on Ryan Farms.

Christmas at the Ryan House in 1999
By: Christina and Whitney Ryan

Christmas at the Ryan House is understandably confusing
After all there are fifteen family members here.
When everyone arrives we meet and greet and seat and eat
While spreading lots of happy Christmas cheer!

Grandma says dinner's ready and we all rush to get in line.
We fill our plates up to the brim with food that's just divine
We sit and eat every bite, mashed potatoes, corn and peas
We forgot the cranberry sauce and pass the rolls please.

The men stuff their faces with turkey and talk about big game,

While the women secretly cheat on their diets and go and hide in shame
It's present time someone shouts and all the kids rush from the den!
Like vultures to a dying cow they snoop and search within.

The adults all take pictures while Tina and Whit play Santa,
The women try to get the lazy men to come on and join us,
In moans and groans they leave the T. V. and complain in chorus.
Well, that's our Ryan Christmas we hope you all had fun,
And remember to keep Christ in Christmas for He's the only one!

Written for sharing time on Christmas Eve

Farewell to Ernest: December 2000

It seems only yesterday we were concerned about entering the new millennium and problems of Y2K. But the transition went smoothly. There have been sad times along with the good times. In April we drove to Tallahassee, Florida to meet our long time friends, Twila and Ed Engler. Johnny was in the service with Ed and it had been 30 years since we had seen them. We had to talk fast over dinner while sharing pictures. Elsanor School received word that the first little one-room school built in 1913 would be marked as a historical building. I was relieved that I had finally finished compiling Elsanor School's history and scrapbooks full of pictures that I had been working on for 2 years. Completing the history and getting a banner and shield for the little school house had been one of my goals since retirement. In October we had to bid my oldest brother, Ernest Dyess, goodbye. Following cancer surgery his heart failed him and he went on to be with the Lord. I miss him terribly since he had been like a father to me and was always concerned about my welfare. Although, his absence leaves a big hole in our hearts we know he fulfilled God's purpose for him while he was on this earth. He had just published his second book *"Divine Appointments,"* so he will live on in his books. I hosted the Elsanor Homemaker's Club ladies' Christmas party at my house in December and Johnny invited his pigeon Club members for supper one night. They seemed to enjoy the crock pot venison with rice and tomato gravy we served for one of the meat dishes.

Merry Christmas to all, the Ryan's of Ryan Roost

2001: We must not take our freedom for granted

Our way of life has changed since we celebrated Christmas last year.
Since the tragedy of September 11, 2001, we now hold our families dearer.
And we think of more important things such as how precious they are,
Not taking our freedom for granted, even though we are in war.

An evil man from a far away land took the security we felt before,
We must even examine the daily mail which appears at our door.
He took innocent lives when the twin towers fell that day
So we remember their families and the heroes when we pray.

How could someone feel such hatred for people they don't even know?
It is because Satan is alive in this world and thinks he is running the show.
But I have news for him, there is someone so much greater than he
Who will let us help the victims and people of Afghanistan go free.

As we celebrate Christmas let Christ reign in your hearts.
He can restore the peace and freedom we had from the start.
As we look at the manger scenes, angels, candles and lights
Think of the only true God who can make everything right!
God Bless the USA with peace from above. Fly your flag. Jeanette and John

2002: The Year of the Fifties,

This has been the year of the fifties as John and I have celebrated our 50th wedding anniversary and also my 50th high school class reunion. Our children and grandchildren hosted a 50th anniversary reception for us at church where we gladly received guests. We had a memorable class reunion. I enjoyed helping in the planning events and also in compiling a booklet of memories of days gone by. We thought we may have to cancel the dinner because of Hurricane Hanna, but it died out late that afternoon. Five of the grandchildren are now teenagers. Christina is attending Judson College and is looking forward to flying to New York City to sing with the Judson Choir at Carnegie Hall this January. Then in the fall they will make a trip to tour England, Scotland and Wales. They will sing in the old cathedrals, churches and schools. Whitney was a contestant in the Mobile Junior Miss program where she won the Fitness award. Her dance performance was awesome. I have started helping one of my friends write the Elsanor Community News for our local newspaper. Our Homemaker Club hosted Christmas and Valentine parties at the new nursing home in Robertsdale this year. Johnny has won a pigeon race or two this year and has ordered an electronic clocking system which clocks the birds the second they fly in the pen. Now he does not have to lose time by catching the birds, taking off their bands and putting them in the old wind-up clock. He built a new pen for his birds which he calls their condominium.

Remember to pray for our President. Jeanette and John

2003 Brought us a new Family Member

One of the big highlights of our year was the marriage of our son, Doyle to Margaret "Maggie" Davidson on July 15, 2003. They met through Doyle's cousin, Bo Dyess when they were teenagers. When Doyle got a chance to visit his Grandpa Dyess at Paxton, Florida, Bo would arrange for Doyle and Maggie to double date with he and his girlfriend, However they both met and married other people. It was over thirty years before Doyle and Maggie saw each other again. Since they were both single they picked up where they left off and were soon married... We are all so happy to have Maggie join our family.

2004 Healing, Protection from Hurricanes and a Trip to Branson

God has been good to us. John had his seed implant for prostate cancer on January 8, 2004, and seems to be doing very well. We pray for a complete recovery. Hurricane Ivan struck us such a blow in September. We have most of the downed trees and debris in the yard cleaned up, and our house now has a new metal roof. Our 40 acres of planted pines are devastated, but John has not decided what to do about that yet. It was an ordeal but we are glad we were protected and are grateful to God for that. One highlight of the year was our vacation with friends to Branson, Missouri in November during Veteran's week. The vets were honored everywhere we went. We enjoyed seeing Andy William's Christmas show, Tony Orlando's play and Ray Steven's cutting up. We changed churches this year and have made new friends but I miss old friends, too. I am enjoying writing a weekly column for the local newspaper. Elsanor Homemaker's Club put a cookbook together of our best recipes. It sold well. It has been a busy year. Love, The Ryan's of Ryan's Roost.

2005 Marriages and a 50th Wedding Anniversaries

We were happy to announce that our oldest granddaughter, Christina graduated Summa Cum Laude from Judson College surrounded by her family and fiancé, Jared Stewart. They were later married on September 17, 2005, in a lovely afternoon ceremony. She will continue her education at UAB Birmingham. Whitney is attending University of South Alabama on scholarships. We are praying for more scholarships for the other grandchildren to help with college expenses when they graduate. The grandchildren helped decorate my house and I have 8 pretty Christmas stockings hanging from the fireplace mantel. My brother, Bernard Dyess and his wife, Ethel, will be celebrating their 50th wedding anniversary in December and I look forward to attending the celebration. I am still busy writing my memories that are published in the newspaper. I pray I get to finish all the stories I have in my mind. Wishing you a Merry Christmas and a Happy New Year, Jeanette and John

2006: Sharing the Fruit

God continues to bless our family. Johnny stayed busy this fall keeping the pecans, lemons, satsumas, and kumquats gathered from the trees and the muscadines from the vines. He picked around 1,735 nice lemons from two trees and also had hundreds of satsumas. He enjoyed sharing his fruit and pecans with friends and relatives. We froze a lot of blueberries for pies and squeezed lemons for juice to freeze for lemonade. We also made a lot of fig preserves and grape jelly. I continue to spend my free time writing historical stories about people who helped shape Baldwin County and my memoirs. I had hoped to put a book together in my life time but time is swiftly passing. Johnny is usually the one who slips and falls, but I had a hard fall on December 19th when I tripped and fell face down on the hard cement of the utility room. I will sport a black eye, gash on my forehead and other bruises on my face for Christmas pictures. Thank God I did not break anything. The grandchildren are busy with school and college. May God bless you and yours and may the year "2007" bring you marvelous joy, blessings and peace.

Love, Jeanette and Johnny

2007: A Poem "At Christmas Time"

At Christmastime I'm thankful for another year
To worship and rejoice with parishioners so dear,
For food and gifts to share with family and friends
My blessings are so many; My list it has no end.

For sunrises, sunsets, butterflies, bluebirds and rain
For the beautiful flowers that bloom in the spring
For warmth in the winter and the breezes of summer
For health and happiness and nighttime slumber

For brave men and women who go off to war
Sacrificing their all for freedom's sake in lands so far,
At Christmas time I pray for love and joy to abound
And that peace throughout this land may be found.

But most of all, I thank God for His great love,
For sending His only Son from above,
For that long ago night when Jesus came as a babe
To bring salvation to all mankind from age to age.

May Christ fill your hearts with joy unspeakable this Christmas. The Ryan's

Blessings 2008:There is a Doctor in the House and a Marketing Major

We are proud that our granddaughter, Whitney Tucker Ryan, graduated Magna Cum Laude from the University of South Alabama with a degree in marketing this spring and is now working in Mobile. She and her fiancé, Orrin Law, have announced their engagement and upcoming marriage in June, 2009. Granddaughter, Christina Stewart received her doctorate degree in Physical Therapy in December and hopes to begin a new job at a hospital in Columbus, MS where she and Jared now live. Our oldest grandson, Joshua Bilon graduated from high school in 2007 and is now attending University of South Alabama on a Mitchell Scholarship. He is seeking a degree in Business. Heather Ryan, our youngest granddaughter also graduated high school in 2007 and is attending Faulkner State on Scholarships. Her sister Hannah Ryan has finished her studies at Faulkner State and has enrolled at Montevallo University. She was most fortunate to meet Donna who invited her to live with her in her home. Hannah was happy to leave the crowded dorm for a spacious bedroom.

2009: Announcing *"Pig Trails and Open Roads"* and *"Faces and Places that live in my Heart"* published in same year.

I have been busy this year attending book signings for my first book that was published in February, 2009 and then compiling stories for my second book that came out in November, 2009. I was very excited to meet old and new friends who stopped by to purchase books. Especially interesting were visits to Rosinton and Elsanor Schools where I discussed my books and local history with students. The stores are selling the books for me and I really appreciate that. Our granddaughter, Heather Ryan and Neal Thompson were married in December so there were showers and teas for her that I enjoyed.

They danced the night away while a band composed of Neal's friends played. Johnny recently had shoulder surgery and is now recuperating. My dreams of compiling a historical book and one of my memoirs has finally materialized and I am blessed to have friends who helped me see the dream come true. Love, Jeanette and John

2010: Book Signings

I was privileged to attend the annual Christmas Bazaar at the PZK Civic Center in Robertsdale on a Saturday in November. I autographed both books for customers and enjoyed visiting with each one. I also sold pear bread, pumpkin bread, pecan pies, muffins and other goodies that I baked which will go toward publishing expenses. I am presently working on a third book, but it may be sometime before it is completed. The cotton on our farm is still waiting for the picker and I see peanuts drying in the sun awaiting the machines in other fields. Harvesting the crops is so much easier now than when my father was a boy and had to stay home from school to pick acres of the prickly cotton bolls. Just think how far we have come since this area was developed and many of us have witnessed it all in our lifetime. I enjoyed Christmas shopping with my girls, (my daughter, Twila and two daughters-in-law, Charlene and Maggie) recently. It has been our tradition to spend one day in November celebrating their birthdays and having lunch together. Twila built on the farm and it is good to have her nearby since we are getting up in age. She helps Johnny take care of the chickens and we now get enough eggs for three families. The lot she lives on is special to her because when she was growing up it served as her pony pasture and later her horse pasture. The farm house was very festive looking this Christmas since I decorated the tree and house with Cardinals. They are my favorite bird and I enjoy watching them as they eat from the bird feeders and splash in the new birdbaths my children gave me for Mother's Day.

Joy, Peace, Love, Jeanette and John

Highlights of 2011 The Year of Graduations

This year has been a year of transition as our grandchildren finished school and college. Hannah graduated Cum Laude from

Montevallo University with a teaching degree. She landed a temporary job teaching third grade when the teacher took leave of absence. Then on June 18, 2011 Hannah and her fiancé, Joshua Meeker were married in a back yard ceremony at her parent's home. The temperature was a little warm during the natural setting ceremony held as the sun was streaming through the trees and sparkling on the green grass, but things cooled during the outdoor reception. Our grandson, Joshua, graduated Magna Cum Laude in May with a degree in Business from University of South Alabama. Later, he received a graduate assistantship scholarship to continue studying for his Master's Degree in Accounting. Sean finished high school in May and has now enrolled at Faulkner Community College, Heather is scheduled to graduate from a college in Mississippi in December and Noah is in the eighth grade in middle school. So with four graduations, a wedding and Twila trying to unpack boxes at her new house life has been busy and the year is not even over.

48
Celebrating Granny's 80th Birthday

Mamie Ethel Ryan is surrounded by her children, Ruth, Elsie and Johnny at her 80th Birthday Party on May 26, 1982

Although Johnny's mother had suffered from crippling arthritis for years and had to walk with a crutch, she continued working in her flowers and living in her trailer next door to us. One evening she asked Doyle to help her move a rose bush. While he was digging the hole in the ground Granny suddenly fell backward fracturing her back. She was admitted to the hospital in a lot of pain. The hospital staff never got her out of bed or administered any therapy for the 15 days she was there so she lost all strength in her legs. Since she could no longer live alone or do for herself she lived with Johnny and me during the summer and with Ruth and Otto when it was time for me to return to work in the fall.

While Granny Ryan was with us after school closed for the summer, I realized that she would be turning 80 on May 26, 1982. I told her Johnny and I wanted to have her an 80th birthday party and invite all her relatives and close friends. Mamie, the youngest of seven children, was born in 1902, so her siblings had all passed away by the time she turned 80. I thought she would be excited and like the idea about a big birthday party so she could see her children and grandchildren as they came to honor her. However, she was not interested in a birthday party. but after a few days she changed her mind and agreed to let us host the party. I quickly began preparing food and punch and ordered a cake from my friend, Betty King, who made the best. I called her old friends at Bethel Church where she attended for many years. Granny worked in the nursery there for several years when the enrollment began to grow. The Sunday morning before the party I stayed home to help her with her bath and to shampoo and roll her hair, as well as prepare an early dinner. Granny was disgruntled and argued that she did not want me to shampoo and roll her hair. I persevered until I had her hair fixed and her best dress on with a corsage pinned to her shoulder. She was happy to greet her children, grandchildren and many local friends. She never acknowledged any thanks or told me she enjoyed the party but I knew she did, especially when her old friend, Mattie Brill came to see her. I did not plan it to receive any credit for myself and I knew there would be no credit given.

Mrs. Ryan passed away in her sleep when she was 83 years old at the Foley Nursing Home. Her children had to admit her when she no longer could get out of bed by herself and we could not lift her. Several of her nieces and nephews from North Alabama, who were her sister's children that she was so close to, came down for her funeral.

In 2010, Mamie and John Ryan's son, John William Ryan, Jr., celebrated his 80th birthday. His children and their spouses honored him with a birthday bash on the Sunday before July 30, 2010. Many of his old and new friends and relatives attended. The house was filled with balloons and streamers and tables laden with refreshments. His cake was decorated with pigeons complete with a pigeon house. His former boss, Lorean Perdue brought him roses, the first he had ever received.

48
Daddy's First Birthday Party

Edward Dyess is pictured with his children and their spouses at his 80th birthday party.

(Left) Ernest and Rachel Dyess, Daddy, Marion and Jeanette Dyess and Jeanette and Johnny Ryan. His son, Bernard and wife, Ethel was unable to attend.

When December of 1982 rolled around, I began to think about the fact that Daddy had never had a planned birthday party where friends and relatives were invited and all the focus was upon him. Sure, I had ordered birthday cakes for him when he was here on his birthday, but it was usually just me and Johnny to help him celebrate. Since Daddy had essential tremors and shook most all the time, a crowd of people made him nervous. That is unless he had something to drink that calmed his nerves and then he was more sociable and ready to talk. He was a simple man and never wanted to be the center of attention, but I was adamant that he deserved an 80th birthday party. I picked out a date close to December 12th and began inviting people and making Christmas goodies. That Sunday the table was laden with all the cookies, candy and snacks I could think of to bake in order to make it a gala event. The relatives and friends came, we visited and reminisced and I was able to keep Daddy in the living room and den most of the time. If guests could not think of something to give him they brought money and a card. There were only two disappointments and that was that his son, Bernard and his wife, Ethel, could not attend because they needed to be at the church Bernard was pastoring. His brother, Willis "Bill" did not feel up to coming either. The next day I heard Daddy telling him on the phone, "Boy, you should have come to my party. I got a billfold full of money for my birthday and a lot of people showed up that I had not seen in a long time." So, even though I had to forge ahead and force my Daddy and Johnny's mother to let me honor them on their 80th birthdays: I know that they found joy knowing others cared for them.

50
The Family Tradition was Broken

Farewell to Daddy, Pop, Grandpa
December 3, 1903
November 25, 1986

Twelve of Daddy's grandchildren attended his funeral. His grandson, Roland "Bo' Dyess was unable to attend. Pictured are, (F): Julie, Twila, Denise, Jonathan, Melissa, Cindy, Gina, (B) Steve, Greg, Doyle and Barry. Present but not pictured is Teresa. His grandsons and granddaughter's spouses served as pall bearers. His children and their spouses are pictured on right: Rachel and Ernest, Ethel and Bernard, Jeanette and George Marion Dyess, Jeanette and Johnny Ryan.

Seven out of the ten Great Grandchildren (at the time) of Edward E. Dyess are: Ashley Dyess, holding Rachel Johnson, Christina Ryan and Amy Dyess holding Christopher Davenport, Back: Brandy and Shawn Nicholson.

Shortly after Mrs. Ryan's passing and her trailer had been cleared of her belongings, except the furniture, I was confronted with a matter that something needed to be done concerning Daddy's situation. Since Daddy had lived about a mile from my brother, Bernard and his wife, Ethel they had seen to his needs by checking on him and by sending him good home cooked meals every day. However, when Bernard was 50 years old he was called to preach, so he turned his farm over to his older son and surrendered to the ministry. Soon he and Ethel were called to pastor a church that they could drive back and forth to on Sundays and Wednesday nights and still live at home. That meant they were still available to see to Daddy's needs and he could help them with their garden. But later when they were called to serve at Victory Baptist Church near DeFuniak Springs, Florida, the church supplied a pastorium for them and they decided to move there in order to be nearer the church. Daddy was then left at his home in the woods without a telephone, and no one to check on him, or take him to buy groceries. He did own an old pick-up truck but along the way his driver's license had expired and he was not supposed to drive on the highway. He only drove it around his place to gather wood and to hunt or over to Bernard's every morning to have coffee with them unless it refused to crank in cold weather.

I felt strongly that since Bernard and Ethel had been there for Daddy for so many years it was now time for me to step up and try to find a solution to Daddy's aloneness. I really wanted to bring him to my house so I could cook for him and take care of his needs but Johnny said that just would not work. Daddy was addicted to alcohol (mostly beer) and he would get something to drink when one of his old friends came by our house to pick him up to visit relatives. Johnny did not like for him to do that and neither did I.

So I began to talk to Daddy about coming to live in the little trailer in our yard that had belonged to Johnny's mother. She had willed it to our son, Doyle, and he said Daddy was welcome to stay there. I hired an electrician to rewire the pole and did a few other improvements before I brought Daddy to Baldwin County. Daddy was somewhat hesitant about the entire arrangement. I realized there could be confusion because Johnny had recently retired from his job at NAS and I was still working so I would not be home during the day.

I never realized what I was doing to Daddy until later. I knew he was nervous and did not want to be in a crowd of people but I did not think about how claustrophobic he was. While I was at work Daddy would come over to our house after he took his morning walk because the trailer was so small. He never learned to make him a cup of coffee on the gas stove.

I never knew exactly what happened between the two of them, but I suppose Johnny needed time to himself. One Sunday as Daddy and I sat in our backyard swing talking, Daddy blurted out, "Nett, It's not working out. You had better just take me back home." I knew he was not happy with the arrangements and he felt as if he was imposing but I was so heartbroken and upset. I did not know what to do. I found out later that he never slept one night in the bed in the trailer but slept on the couch in the living room. Two men coming and going in the same house turned out to be as big a problem as two women trying to get along. That evening sitting in the swing set was probably the first time I saw my Daddy cry and I cried with him. I told Daddy I wished he would stay because I could take care of him but he never wanted to be a burden on anyone.

Early the following Saturday we loaded up his few things and left for his home in the woods. We had to face other problems when he got home. He had been having trouble with his pump and his old truck. I bought him some groceries, but knew he would not try to cook much. He just never had the desire to learn to cook. I cleaned his house and cooked a good dinner before leaving for home on Sunday. I cried all the way home as the sadness of the memory of Daddy waving to me as I drove off leaving him there alone in his yard by himself. I prayed I would not get a call from his neighbor's family who sometimes visited him telling me they found Daddy dead in his house.

In September of 1985, I received a letter from Daddy. He had written it in his shaky sprawling handwriting. As I made out the words I thought his penmanship was fairly good considering he was only granted a fourth grade education. Today, as I hold the letter in my hands I read that they had a good garden that summer and that he picked the vegetables for Ethel. He seems proud that he contributed to the filling of her freezer. I read on and once more grasp his loneliness and regret the trouble he had sleeping at night due to a stomachache. On the next line he apologizes for telling me his problems by stating that he is alright in other ways, so he is not complaining. He tells me that his grandson, Greg, came up and took him fishing. They caught a fine mess of fish that Greg fried for dinner and how good they were. On the next page he writes that Ernest came by and that they talked it over and he wants to have Thanksgiving again at his place in November. As I read Daddy's letter tonight on September of 2011, the tears start flowing. Daddy's last request to me was, "Look girl, if you will come up and help me one more time so we can get together one last Thanksgiving I won't ask you again. I will do all I can to help you. Write and tell me if you can help me out and I won't ask you no more. But I am pretty sure this will be my last one anyway." The letter ended, "Look girl, you are the only girl I got and I think a lot of you." He never voiced it in his letter, but I knew what he meant. He just did not know how to say, "I love you."

I had been going up on Tuesdays before Thanksgiving and with record breaking speed I cleaned his house from top to bottom. I always changed the bed sheets and then we would drive to the laundromat in Florala to wash and dry his clothes. After I cleaned his refrigerator we would stop on our way back and buy groceries. Daddy was always responsible for raking and cleaning the yards and filling his big wood box so we would have plenty of wood for his small fireplace.

I immediately answered his letter. I told him that I would drive up the Tuesday before the holidays and help him out. We did indeed celebrate the holiday that year together as a family. The men enjoyed deer hunting as usual and the women cooked their special dishes. I really wanted to bring Daddy to my house but he had started getting a supplemental check from the government to help with his small Social Security check so he was supposed to live alone. After the holidays I rented him a drafty older house in my community so I could drive over and see him every day after work. He was terribly lonesome and cold in that big house as we waited for a modern apartment for him in the Loxley Senior apartment complex where his brother, Willis lived. I prayed for a quick vacancy to open in the senior citizen's apartment but I was very upset with myself because

I did not bring Daddy to my house until he got an apartment. He eventually lost the small government check anyway when he sold his house to my brother and he had the right to live there as long he lived. I even explained it to the judge but we lost the case.

So I made the second trip to bring Daddy back to Baldwin County from his house in the woods to live near me. As we drove off he looked wistfully at his home and said, "I will never live to see another Thanksgiving." He was 82 years old and still in fairly good health, so I rebuked him and told him not to talk like that because we could celebrate Thanksgiving at one of our homes." He made no other comment. It was as if he was resigned to the fact that our 35-year-old family tradition was coming to a close and he would not be with us for another Thanksgiving holiday.

In April the apartment manager called me and said he had Daddy an available apartment not far from Uncle Bill's. The week before I was to drive up to bring his things to Baldwin County I broke out with painful shingles on my face so Johnny and Daddy had to go by themselves. The next week when I felt better we got Daddy settled in the apartment. Every Wednesday after I got off work at Rosinton School, I drove over to Loxley to clean his apartment with the new vacuum cleaner we bought with money he had saved. We also purchased a new color television set so he could watch the baseball games. I had a telephone installed thinking he would call me or one of my brothers when he wanted to talk or needed something. That never happened. He would answer the phone when we called but never made a call as far as I know. While there, I hurried to the grocery store, that Daddy's former sister-in-law, Dora Belle Dyess Steele ran, to pick up his groceries and then cook him some supper. He always wanted cornbread and began to only eat cornbread and milk because when I went back to see him he had not eaten the other food I left. While I was hurrying around washing his dishes and cleaning I always encouraged Daddy to take his bath so I could bring his dirty clothes home with me to wash. When I had finished with the house work and had his bills paid I left for prayer meeting at my church. I thought I needed to be at church every time the doors opened, but now I know that God would have forgiven me if I had sat down and talked to Daddy and kept him company for awhile since he was so lonely and was going through such a dramatic change in his life.

As much as we enjoyed our family gatherings, we realized all good things must come to an end in due time. Family traditions must be broken. I knew Daddy was not happy having to leave the place that had been home to him for so many years. Just as we were making plans to go to my brothers in Camden for our get-together on the Tuesday before Thanksgiving, I got the call at work. Daddy had stepped out of his apartment early that morning to take his neighbor's garbage to the bin and suddenly fell dead. He had suffered a massive heart attack. We buried him not far from the place of his birth near Rosinton on the day before the Thanksgiving holiday. As I mourned his death, it suddenly dawned on me that Daddy knew what he was talking about the year before. It was not meant to be that he would spend Thanksgiving anywhere else but at his old home place in the woods.

When I talked to him on the phone on Monday night to tell him I would pick him up Tuesday morning to take him to the doctor he said he had a little indigestion, but I did not realize it could be his heart causing him to feel dizzy. If he was hurting he never told me. He was almost 83 years old and had never spent one night in the hospital and he did not intend to break his record so he told me he was feeling alright. We cancelled our plans to have Thanksgiving at Ernest and Rachel's and the family all came to my house for Daddy's funeral. We buried him next to Mama on a country road in Rosinton. All of his children and 12 of his 13 grandchildren and seven of his ten great-grandchildren attended his funeral. That year our family Thanksgiving tradition was broken. Our families would never again celebrate Thanksgiving as we had in the past 35 years. It would now be up to me and my brothers to begin our own holiday traditions with our children and grandchildren. Thanksgiving would no longer be the wonderful, joyous time when all of Daddy's offspring met for three or four days in the woods. There would be no more quail, dove or deer hunts for the men of the family to enjoy. No more bragging and discussions about which one of their favorite teams would win in the Iron Bowl as they listened on truck radios in a dove field. Most of the men were Auburn fans since Ernest attended Auburn, but Pop,

Johnny and our boys rooted for Alabama. The women of the family would not be able to pitch in by chopping ingredients for Rachel's large roaster full of dressing and giblet gravy. There would be no more exchanges of recipes or a time to catch up on the latest happenings in each others lives. There would certainly not be any reason for me to think about celebrating a joyous Thanksgiving the next day after all my family members returned to their homes. Instead of cooking, I would spend the day shedding tears as I cleaned out the few belongings Daddy had acquired in this life, which was not much. There would be no joy in my heart to share the next day, but from time to time I would stop and thank God for allowing my family to share the best blessings of the past with a father who loved us all. He helped us build and repair our houses and pick our gardens for us, but never asked for anything or complained no matter what came his way. He had taught his sons and grandsons so much about the techniques of hunting, fishing and other things of nature. Sometimes it takes death to realize the worth of a person. When I was a teenager I only thought about Daddy's faults and was ashamed of his habits at times. Now I think of his gentle nature, his disdain for arguments or confusion and his unconditional love even if he could not express it. I often reminisce of those happy days gone by that I can only dream of now.

Pa-Pa

On Wednesday he was laid to rest
Time had come for his life test
Believing in his heart, he had done his best
No grudges, no ill-will buried in his chest

Oh, so many memories we all recall
The wonderful things he did, big and small
Most being big and good, from our heart never fall
We will never forget them, no, not one at all

Gardens he planted and worked by his hand
All will agree the best in the land

With his old worn out hoe he never paused to stand
He just kept after the grasses very last stand.

Arising early to go fishing on Blackwater creek
The very best event of the week
Pole and bait in hand what a shine on his cheek,
Just to know so much fun was his to seek.

Thanksgiving Day a very special time
All his children arriving at his home safe and fine,
With all the grandchildren in their prime,
Seated around the dinner table, faces shine.

The Lord so gracious gave him 82 years. a bountiful life,
His passing leaves our hearts as though they've been pierced with a knife,
Our prayer, our hope, that he's where there's no trouble or strife,
And that he's communing with Jesus and Lola, his wife.

Pa-Pa, Pa-Pa, the greatest Pa-Pa of all,
Our hearts are warmed by how he stood so tall,
Small in statue, but a heart soft as a foam ball,
Time cannot erase our memories whether big or small.
Ethel H. Dyess
Written: November 30, 1986

51
The Year of the Fifties

Jeanette and Johnny Celebrating their 50ᵗʰ Wedding Anniversary.

Jeanette pictured with members of her Sunday school class at Bethel Baptist Church who helped serve.

One by one the years flew by so quickly. Our children had been on their own for many years but we remained as active as possible and were looking forward to celebrating our fiftieth wedding anniversary. We were not sure just how we would mark the day until our children decided that they would honor us by hosting a reception for us at Bethel Baptist Church where we had attended for approximately 50 years.

Since they were busy with family and work, I volunteered to pick out some of the decorations. I found stems of magnolias and magnolia branches at a local store so I had a theme. I took the flowers to an old friend who was in her nineties but was still arranging flowers. She made the beautiful floral arrangements for me in gold stem vases. Golden candle holders encircled with magnolia blossoms and greenery became the table centerpieces. A decorated wooden trellis provided the background for the beautiful 50ᵗʰ anniversary cake made especially for us by my good friend, Betty King. She also made the groom's cake and loaned me her candles decorated with magnolias. Johnny stopped at a neighbor's and I asked if he would mind if I broke off a few magnolia branches from the low hanging limbs of his tree. He told me to take all I wanted.

I placed the large bouquet of flowers in the sanctuary for the morning services and two others on long tables where I displayed old wedding gifts that were treasures we managed to keep all those years. There was the delicate burgundy colored lamp that Aunt Effie Mae Mixon had given me at one of my showers and the cake plate with matching burgundy tea pot and sugar and creamy bowls that my friend, Sarah gave me. One item that I had never used, a lovely glass serving dish with a dip container all encircled with gold trim, which was a gift from my next door neighbors, the Postles.

Granny Ryan had given us a flower garden quilt top and lining for a wedding present that had been in the linen closet wrapped in moth balls in the first house and then in plastic in a cedar lined closet later. I wondered why she never offered to quilt it for us because I did not know how to quilt, but perhaps she did not quilt either. However after washing the hand sewed quilt some of the small octagon shaped pieces came apart and had to be repaired. I took it to Mrs. Young in Styx River who repaired and quilted it beautifully. I not only displayed it at our anniversary reception but the quilt, now hanging on a quilt rack is one of my prized possessions today. I also displayed the delicate bone china tea set that Bernard sent us from Germany while he was stationed there. Then there was a wooden bowl that Johnny refers to as his popcorn bowl that his Aunt Grace Ryan gave us and the rather bent-up baking pans Aunt Annie Edwards sent us. I would never forget the aluminum mixing bowl with one handle our cousins, Willie and Claude purchased at Lovemans in Birmingham where Willie worked. I have used this bowl consistently every day and do not think I could make cornbread or cookies without it. I used gold matching frames to put our black and white wedding pictures in so I could place them on the table for display. The anniversary cake was topped with the same bride and groom that had adorned our first wedding cake 50 years ago. Doyle had the food catered and I baked a table full of goodies. The ladies of my Sunday school class and our grandchildren helped serve. Twila designed the programs and sang a song she wrote for us titled, "*I Am Blessed*." Barry welcomed the approximately 150 guests and Doyle also said a few words. As we cut the anniversary cake a friend, Julia Frisk sang our favorite songs, "The Rose" and "Wind Beneath My Wings." We dearly missed our granddaughter, Christina, who was on a mission trip and could not be present. Our anniversary pictures were incomplete without her smiling face.

The highlight of the day was to be able to speak with relatives from both sides of our families. My cousins brought Aunt Ora Mae Shumock Mills, who was Mama's only living sibling. There were nieces, nephews and many cousins from different states who attended. Besides our church and community friends there were members of Johnny's pigeon club who came and school classmates of mine. It was indeed a memorable day for us.

Conclusion

Time has evolved and everything has changed as the years passed. The little house down the lane built out of logs in the forties that held so many memories, no longer stands. We sold the property years ago. The new owner decided he wanted to do away with the house so it was burned. As I drove down the road after attending prayer meeting one night I saw the fire and I had sad feelings. It had been our home for 15 years, but I had not visited it since we moved because I wanted to remember it like we left it. Only memories of the little gray house where our children were born remains.

Our three children grew up, married and gave us seven wonderful grandchildren who continue to make us proud. Christina, Whitney, Hannah, Joshua and Heather have graduated college with honors and they either have jobs or continue working on other degrees. All four of our granddaughters are married to men of faith and character and we enjoy their visits when they come for family gatherings. Sean enrolled in Jr. College last fall and Noah attends middle school.

Since Johnny and I are older we can no longer travel very far or do some of the things we did in the past. We are pretty content and thankful that he can still drive the tractor for a few hours a day and that we are able to attend church services and events. My daylilies, larkspur, phlox and four o'clock's popup every spring and bloom profusely, along with our 75 Crepe Myrtles and other flowers, although I am not able to pull weeds. I enjoy watching the butterflies, humming birds and bumble bees as they gather nectar from the flowers, and the cardinals and other species of birds that eat from the feeders and splash in the birdbaths.

A few things have not changed since we moved into this 43-year-old farmhouse. I still enjoy cooking for family gatherings. Our family continues celebrating Christmas together at our home each year although now the girls lend a hand preparing dinner. I try to think of a different decorating theme each year. The Christmas tree is now artificial instead of the lop-sided cedars we had so much fun looking for in the woods. The decorations are more brilliant since the house sparkled with the color of red cardinals and greenery last year.

If I could sum up my life with just a few words; they would be: blessed, loved, fulfilled, content, rewarding and much too short. It seems that the years rolled by, one by one, until here I am in the latter part of my life. One day I was a child going through the motions of daily living. I remember looking at older people and thinking that it would be a long, long time before I would be their age. Then time carried me and my pride through the invincible teenage years and the fast paced young adult years. I must have just blinked when all of a sudden I was in my middle-years when my eyes began to play tricks on me and aches and pains started calling much too often. Retirement came much too soon and now I can barely remember the strong productive years before I was categorized as a retired senior citizen. I recall the day when I would not acknowledge being in that category with a group of "Young at Hearts" because I thought I was much too young at age 55.

Then one day I woke up to the fact that the days, months and years I was privileged to have lived, loved and laughed on this earth had added up to 70. I was reminded by my peers over and over again that I was now living on "borrowed time." They stated that the Bible says that we are not promised more than three score and ten years. I passed 70 a few years ago. Now seven years later, when I wake up in the morning I thank God for giving me another day of life. I hesitate to call the years "Golden Years." I read where an older person wrote that they were in the winter of their life. I realize that I have many more summers behind me than I have ahead of me.

With that in mind I wanted to write down these short stories of the daily incidents and happenings of an average family living on a small farm in rural South Alabama. Most of the stories concern happy tales about our children and their adventures fishing, hunting and learning responsibility or happy days of horseback riding and finding wild animals to tame as pets. Some stories tell of unhappy relationships and others are sad as we had to let go of loved ones whose death broke family traditions. Life for me was not always easy because of situations beyond my control, yet I struggled to find a happy medium and enjoy the good times such as the accomplishments of my children and grandchildren. I hoped to provide a positive home life for them in times of turmoil. I tried to dedicate my life to the service of my Lord and Savior and depend on Him for comfort when I was lonely or downhearted. God has never let me down and is always there for me when I need Him.

I believe God has a purpose for my time on earth and has fulfilled my dreams by allowing me to write down some of the true stories concerning hardships, hard work and hard times when it was not easy to care for my family. I now wish to leave my minute mark of my legacy of a servant's heart and desire to leave this world a better place than I found it. I admit that I made many wrong choices and mistakes. I did not always use the best judgment at times or was I always obedient to God's voice, but in time those things will be erased. I pray my offspring will do their part to love the Lord thy God with all their heart, soul and mind and their neighbor as themselves, as they journey through life. This is my fervent prayer and my ever present dream. They are a small part of my being and I pray for God to guide them as they experience the miracle of life.

Until we meet again, Jeanette

The Ryan Family in December of 2009

John and Jeanette, their children, spouses and grandchildren are
pictured at the wedding of Heather Ryan and Neal Thompson. Front
and Back: Whitney and Orrin Law, Maggie and Doyle Ryan, Noah
Ryan, Christina and Jared Stewart, Sean Ryan, Heather and Neal
Thompson, Barry and Charlene Ryan, Hannah Ryan Meeker, Josh
Bilon, Jeanette and John Ryan and Chris and Twila Bilon. Not pictured
is Josh Meeker.